Called to Life

Called to Life

Jacques Philippe

Translated by Neal Carter

 Scepter

Originally published as *Appelés á la vie*
Copyright © 2008, Editions des Beatitudes, S.O.C.
Burtin, France

English translation copyright © 2008
Scepter Publishers, Inc.
P.O. Box 211, New York, N.Y. 10018
www.scepterpublishers.org
All rights reserved.

ISBN-13: 978-1-59417-069-0

To my family.

To my brothers and sisters of the Beatitude Community.

I thank all the people whose comments and encouragement helped me in the writing of this book, in particular:

Xavier Lacroix, Jean-Claude Sagne,
Sr. Déborah, Sr. Catherine of Siena,
Sr. Marie-Pia, Sr. Marie-Noël.

CONTENTS

··3··

The Word of God and Its Power to Call / 30

··4··

Life's Events / 56

·· 5 ··

Obedience to Others and to the Holy Spirit / 89

Conclusion / 102

Appendix

Practical Advice for *Lectio Divina* / 109

INTRODUCTION

How do I find fulfillment in life? How do I obtain happiness? How do I fully become a man or woman? These perennial questions are increasingly asked in today's directionless world, where no one accepts ready-made solutions and people must find answers on their own. Resistant to standards imposed from outside, most people in practice try to make the most of life and construct happiness according to their own understanding of it. The ideal of happiness comes from their own education and experience, but, whether they notice it or not, is also strongly shaped by mainstream culture and the media. Usually such happiness is fragile—unable to stand up under sicknesses, failures, separations, and the various trials we all encounter. Then life seems not to have kept the promises it made us in our youth.

Yet, I believe human life is a marvelous adventure. Despite the burden of sufferings and disappointments, it offers us means to grow in humanity, freedom, and interior peace, while exercising our entire capacity for love and joy.

There is, however, one condition. We must give up our own agendas and allow ourselves to be led by life, in happy events and difficult ones, while learning to recognize and accept the calls addressed to us day by day.

"Call" is the keyword of this book. The idea, simple but very meaningful, is absolutely fundamental to our temporal and spiritual plans. Human beings cannot attain fulfillment solely by carrying out their own projects. These projects are legitimate and necessary, and we must bring our intelligence and energy to bear on accomplishing them. But that's not enough, and in the event of failure it can lead to disillusionment. Another attitude, one in the end more decisive and fruitful, must accompany our initiating and carrying out of projects: that of listening to the calls, the discrete, mysterious invitations that come to us continuously throughout life. This attitude of listening and availability takes priority over even the projects themselves. I believe we can be fulfilled as human beings only to the extent that we perceive and respond to the calls life addresses to us day in and day out: calls to change, grow, mature, enlarge our hearts and our horizons, and leave behind hardness of heart and narrow-mindedness in order to welcome reality in a larger and more confident manner.

These calls come to us in many ways. Sometimes they come through experiences or by the example of others who touch us, sometimes from desires that arise in our hearts or requests from people who are close to us, often from Holy Scripture. They originate from

God, who gives us life, never ceases to watch over us, and wants tenderly to lead and constantly intervene for each of his children in a way that is discreet, often imperceptible, yet efficacious. Although many are, unfortunately, unaware of this presence and action of God, they reveal themselves to those who know how to place themselves in the attitude of listening and availability.

God is the God of the living, not the dead. He reaches out to us continually, mysteriously but certainly, infusing our lives with value, beauty, and fruitfulness beyond our imagining. As St. Paul said:

> Now to him who by the power at work within us is able to do far more abundantly than all that we ask or think, to him be glory in the church and in Christ Jesus to all generations, for ever and ever. Amen. (Eph 3:20–21).

How sad it would be to cut oneself off from God's action and bury oneself in the narrow, illusory world of one's own projects.

Behind the many calls addressed to us in life there is but one call—God's. It takes its fullest and most luminous form in the mystery of Christ. In perceiving and responding to this call, human beings realize their humanity and discover authentic happiness, a happiness that will be fully theirs in the glory of the life to come. In his letter to the Ephesians, St. Paul speaks of the extraordinary hope that God's call in Christ opens to us:

> I do not cease to give thanks for you, remembering you in my prayers, that the God of our Lord Jesus Christ, the Father of glory, may give you a spirit of wisdom and of revelation in the knowledge of him, having the eyes of your hearts enlightened, that you may know what is the hope to which he has called you, what are the riches of his glorious inheritance in the saints, and what is the immeasurable greatness of his power in us who believe, according to the working of his great might (Eph 1:16–19).

In the pages that follow I mean to show the importance and fruitfulness of this idea, then to discuss some areas where divine calls are frequently encountered: major events of life, the Word of God (subject of a long chapter), and the desires that the Spirit awakens in our hearts.

I shall insist that any call from God is a call to life. Our first vocation is to live, and a call cannot be from God unless it leads us to live in a more intense and beautiful way, engaging human life as it is with more confidence, in all its aspects: physical, psychological, emotional, intellectual, and spiritual.

But let me conclude this introduction by speaking of the potential reader of this book. I treat the idea of being called in a Christian context and with a Christian vocabulary because I am convinced that the most profound and enlightening words ever pronounced on the human condition can be found in the Bible and especially in the Gospels. But anyone will find here much that is valuable. To be called is fundamental to the human condition.

Finally, a word about *responsibility, freedom, desire.*

Responsibility presupposes the existence of a call, of a duty. To take responsibility for one's actions is not only to accept responsibility for their impact on others, but to acknowledge that one had several options— good or bad as the case may be—before choosing and acting. Even so, to give the idea of *freedom* real weight requires recognition of some kind of call. The exercise of human freedom is arbitrary and trivial unless it is a response to an invitation from something that transcends it. As for *desire*, it becomes a mere psychological construct, a product of the alchemy of impulse unless understood at the deepest level as a call. Beneath the often contradictory desires of the human heart lies a single desire—for fulfillment, for happiness. To show it respect as something serious, something fully human, and not simply one more craving or impulse, we must see in it the traces of a call that comes from beyond ourselves.

Humanity cannot be understood apart from a call to become more human. Where does it come from?

What is its source? This is the fundamental question of life. I take my stand in the Christian camp, but I believe the following reflections have something to say to any person of good will.

·· 1 ··

MAN: ESSENTIALLY
A CALLED BEING

Mankind's defining aspect is his capacity to hear the call of God.[1]

BIBLICAL AND ANTHROPOLOGICAL
IMPORTANCE OF A CALLING

One of Pope John Paul II's key affirmations, made during a series of catechetical discourses on marriage early in his pontificate, calls attention to the fact that human beings, although marked by sin, are on a deeper level persons who have been called.

> The analysis of Christ's words from the Sermon on the Mount [. . .] leads us to the conviction that the human heart is not so much accused and condemned by Christ because of concupiscence as it is first and above all called. There is a clear divergence here

[1] Jean-Claude Sagne, *Les sacrements et la vie spirituelle* (Paris: Médiaspaul, 2007), 57.

between the anthropology of the Gospel and influential representatives of contemporary hermeneutics (what we will call masters of suspicion).[2]

The notion of call is fundamental. It is at the heart of the biblical vision of man and clearly separates a vision faithful to the Gospel from one foreign or opposed to it.

First, the theme of a God who manifests himself to mankind and invites a response is present throughout the Scriptures, as much in the Old Testament as in the New. Consider the numerous stories of vocation from the Old Testament—Abraham, Moses, Samuel, Isaiah, Jeremiah.[3] These are among the Bible's most beautiful passages, because they reveal the personal character of the relationship between God and man. They show the fragility and hesitance of humankind and also our availability—our capacity to say yes. God's sovereignty is manifest here together with his merciful tenderness toward his creature. Especially we see what God's intervention can bring to the forefront of a life, the unpredictable and surprising paths that can spring up, the fruitfulness that God can bestow on us.

And of course many of the people in the New Testament are aware that the deepest meaning of their lives has come to them by God's call through Christ. To

[2] Catechesis of February 9, 1983.
[3] Gen. 12:1–15; Ex 3:1–20; 1 Sam 3:1–20; Isa 6:1–13; Jer 1:1–10.

take just one example: this is a fundamental theme for St. Paul. He is aware that all value of his life comes entirely from the call he received on the road to Damascus. All grace, all life, all fruitfulness, all moral authenticity depends on responding to God's call. Paul speaks about this often, either citing his own experience or exhorting the communities he tends to be faithful to God's call through Christ. As in this:

> Paul, called by the will of God to be an apostle of Christ Jesus, and our brother Sosthenes, to the church of God which is at Corinth, to those sanctified in Christ Jesus, called to be saints together with all those who in every place call on the name of our Lord Jesus Christ, both their Lord and ours: Grace to you and peace from God our Father and the Lord Jesus Christ (1 Cor 1:1–2).

This notion of a call in a sense gives unity to the whole of Scripture. Beyond the diversity of authors, times, styles, and ways of thinking, all the books of the Bible witness to the same fundamental spiritual experience: God speaks with mankind, proposing a way of life and awaiting a free response.

From an anthropological point of view, that mankind is called is not some remote reality, something that happens only from time to time or reserved, as might wrongly be supposed, for certain privileged individuals who are fortunate enough to receive a special vocation. Rather than being added to our natural makeup, as if it were something we could get along without, calling is basic to our very identity as human persons. The fullness of human flourishing is not possible by the use only of our own physical, intellectual, psychic, and emotional resources. We can only fully realize our humanity by responding to God's calls—subtle and mysterious, to be sure, yet also real and constant all during our lives.

MEDITATION AND FORMS OF CALLING

God's calls are not direct, like a telephone call; they come through meditation, which I will say more of later. We can attend to Holy Scripture (the Word of God is a powerful medium), to the events of our life, to certain encounters, to requests of friends or superiors, and even to the internal invitations of the Holy Spirit and the desires of our hearts.[4] God never ceases to speak with us in such ways, inviting us to make progress in one way or another, while at the same time giving us the necessary grace and strength.

God's call can concern important life choices and be a vocation in the classic sense (a vocation to the

[4] There is a Trinitarian aspect to the three principle axes of our meditations: the providence of the Father (in events), the Word of the Son, and the inspirations of the Spirit.

consecrated life, to marriage, to a p[...]
the Church or in society). Often, th[...]
receive from God bear upon small[...]
an invitation to pardon, an act of co[...]
cult situation, a service to rend[...]
moment of prayer. . . . It is as import[...]
calls and consent to them, for, small as they may seem,
they mark out the path that leads to a far richer and
more abundant life than we would otherwise know.
Every yes to God's call, even in the least matter, brings
an increase of life and strength and encouragement,
for God gives himself to those who are open to his calls
and confers ever more freedom upon them.

THE CALL, PATH OF FREEDOM

"*For you were called to freedom, brethren*" (Gal 5:13). So says
St. Paul in the letter to the Galatians. God calls us to freedom. But instead of being given to us instantaneously
and in full measure, this freedom is built up progressively
and patiently day by day, by being faithful to God's calls.
Typically, they open a space of freedom in us whereby we
can escape the various snares that so easily engulf us. Let
us consider this from several perspectives.

Unless called, human beings remain *enclosed in
their sin.*

As the story in Genesis of creation and the fall
makes clear, sin is a rejection of life as God's child

ging enslavement with it. Through pride, human
eings refuse to accept life and happiness from the
Father's hands, with confident and loving dependency,
preferring to be the source of life for themselves.
Suspicions, fears, worries, and inflamed desires are the
result. Looking for happiness not to God, but to ourselves, we feverishly seek it in things like riches, pleasure, and fame. Our state of being called points to a
path of liberation from some of the most fundamental
expressions of sin: pride, fear, and desire.

Openness to God's calls frees us from *pride*. It
sweeps aside the attitude of self-sufficiency, the pre-
tense that one is the sole master of one's life. In its
place come dependency, availability to another, humility, and confident submission. Openness to God's calls
helps us escape the pitfalls of *desire*. God redirects
desire toward goods better able to satisfy us than those
we lust after. And this openness frees us from fear. By
being open to God's calls, the believer receives encouragement and strength that empower him to rise above
his fears and break out of the narrow circle of inade-
quate coping strategies by which people too often
attempt to handle fear.

When the Pharisees in the Gospels are scandalized at
seeing Jesus eat with tax collectors and sinners, Jesus
replies: *I have not come to call the righteous to repentance but
sinners* (Lk 5:32). Here is the infinite mercy of God, who
calls us not because of our merits but purely out of love.

He does not want us to remain prisoners of our past. He always wants to propose a new future to us, however hesitant we may be. The best way to leave sin and misery behind is not by despairing or blaming ourselves, but by opening up to God's calls that come to us continually, no matter what our situation is. Even the most hardened sinner is called. And the call is a path of salvation for him.

Unless called, we remain *trapped within our own psyches*—their suggestions, impulses, and imaginings. The natural functioning of the human psyche, and its complex world of emotions and images, is valuable, indeed indispensable, a fundamental link between the person and his surroundings. But it has its limits. It is capable of isolating us, all the more so because of its fundamental tendency to protect identity and assure survival. Access to the richness of reality can be impaired by the limitations, and sometimes the dysfunctions, of feelings and imagination. The psychological representations of reality may distort true beauty. Unlike reality itself, the representations of reality can imprison us, and our emotions may be out of balance with the facts, leaving us indifferent to very important realities and greatly exercised over trivia.

In particular, our image of happiness—our psychological representation of what we consider possible and think will make us happy—is often only distantly related to real, satisfying happiness. This is the human tragedy: to seek to realize an image of happiness proposed to us by the surrounding culture and our psyches, without ever finding true happiness. Today, more than ever we strive to master and control life, realize our projects, satiate our (legitimate) thirst for happiness, without understanding that we often are imprisoned by the limitations of what the psyche can comprehend and desire and its failure to grasp where our true happiness lies.

While the mental and emotional representations that direct our lives are partially true, very often they are limited and misleading. They must undergo a constant conversion, an opening up to the richness of reality as God has made it, vaster and far more fruitful than any mental construct. As St. Paul says:

> As it is written: "What no eye has seen, nor ear heard, nor the heart of man conceived, what God has prepared for those who love him" (1 Cor 2:9).

Sorrow and renunciation, struggle and agony are part of the opening up to reality. This is a work in progress, never complete here on earth that makes possible for us an ever more abundant and fulfilling life.

OPENNESS TO THE FUTURE

Responding to God opens new, unpredictable horizons. Here is the future, no matter what our past or present may be. Here also is an immense gift, for there is nothing worse than to be without a future. Uprisings by young people in disadvantaged areas in France, however unacceptable in some ways, are testimony to the profound hopelessness that comes with feeling that society offers them no future.

That said, it is important to understand that God's calls do not always involve the whole future panorama of one's life. Sometimes one is called to take just a single little step—"nothing except for today," as St. Thérèse of Lisieux said.[5] But it is enough to live and advance a day at a time, finding meaning in existence and persevering until one receives the grace to see more. In fact, it is better that we not know the future but discover it step by step. We are tempted to imagine that security lies in mastering the future, but the reverse is true: the more we confidently entrust the future to God, without trying to know it or master it, the more secure and peaceful we are.

Moreover—and this too is extremely important—a call liberates us by permitting us to live out the situation in which we find ourselves in a positive way. Even if what happens to us seems chaotic at times and hard to understand, *everything we face contains a call from God.*

Happy events are invitations to give thanks. Regrettable events are invitations to faith, hope, and conversion. Openness to God's calls unifies life and enables

---

[5] St. Thérèse of Lisieux, Poem number 5.

us to transcend the hard knocks that come with living. I shall return to this subject later.

EVERY CALL IS CREATIVE

God's first call to us, the root and foundation of the rest, is the call to being. In the Letter to the Romans St. Paul speaks of "*God . . . who gives life to the dead and calls into existence the things that do not exist*" (Rom 4:17). The fact that we do exist is a response of a sort, but we are invited to continue responding throughout life. All God's calls resemble this first one in that they draw us out of nothingness, out of meaninglessness, out of isolation, in order to make us more fully alive.

CALLING AND OFFERING

God's calls are fruitful because they carry with them the grace to respond. In asking us to follow one or another path, God also gives us the necessary strength and grace. God is faithful, and he gives what he commands, as St. Augustine puts it.

Furthermore, whenever life offers us a gift—a moment of happiness, a friendship, a chance to do something worthwhile—the gift contains an implicit call: an invitation to give thanks for the gift received, to welcome it fully, to make it productive for ourselves and others, to make ourselves totally available to God's action. "There is no truly profitable gift from God except for him who recognizes it as a gift and chooses to welcome it without reserve."[6]

Calling and gift are two complementary faces of the same reality: the act by which God infuses us with rich, abundant, and fruitful life whose potential is unfolded by our free consent.

Openness to the call is openness to the fullness of life. Not only natural, physical, emotional, and intellectual life, but also the life realized through relationships, love, communion and, ultimately, through participation in divine, supernatural life. Every call is a call to love more and find fulfillment by participating in the purity and ardor of divine love.

LOSING ONESELF TO FIND ONESELF

Only the notion of calling makes it possible accurately to express both the legitimate desire for self-realization and the evangelical summons to self-renunciation.

Self-realization and personal development are highly prized values today. Libraries are filled with countless works outlining techniques, good and bad, to achieve these things. The desire is legitimate. But it is not so easy to reconcile it with the language of the

---

[6] Sagne, *Les sacraments et la vie spirituelle*, 52. This work contains very beautiful passages on the notion of calling.

Gospels, which seems to urge renunciation and abnegation. Believers cannot simply ignore Jesus' words:

> If any man would come after me, let him deny himself and take up his cross and follow me. For whoever would save his life will lose it; and whoever loses his life for my sake and the Gospel's will save it (Mk 8:34–35).

We also cannot ignore a saying like that of Thérèse of Lisieux who exclaimed, "If we knew what we earn in renouncing all things!"[7] The truth of this has to be understood and integrated into any authentic spiritual way.

The Cross will always be a challenge, but at least this is true: The question at issue here cannot even be addressed apart from the dynamic of call-and-response. The Gospel's words on self-renunciation quoted above are to be understood in relation to the proclamation of the Kingdom and the call addressed to those who come after Jesus to place availability to the good news of the Kingdom before everything else.

In responding to God's calls we simultaneously lose and find ourselves in an authentically Christian way. There is nothing unhealthy or perverse about it. Our "loss" is not self-destruction or masochism but a coming

---

[7] Sr. Geneviève, *Conseils et souvenirs* (Cerf), coll. Foi vivante, 131.

out of oneself and one's limits so as to be more fully open to life. The "discovery" is not a narcissistic and egoistic self-seeking but access to our most profound identity as children of God—an identity at once revealed and given to us as we respond to the calls that come to us constantly throughout life.

•• 2 ••

OUR VOCATION AS
CREATED BEINGS

I want to emphasize a point that to me seems essential. The most fundamental call addressed to us is the call to live. God's first gift to us is the gift of life, and this gift is already a vocation.

While preaching retreats sometimes I ask this question: What is the first great gift that God has given us? Often, the response is: Baptism. But although baptism is indeed a marvelous gift that gives us access to the riches of Trinitarian life, God's very first gift is human life!

It is understandable that people often have difficulty in welcoming life as a gift. Life brings sorrows, sufferings, and disappointments. Sometimes we feel that it is more a burden than a gift. Didn't Job curse the day he came into the world? *"Let the day perish wherein I was born, and the night which said, 'A man-child is conceived'"*

(Job 3:3). But even with its trials and sufferings, life still is a gift.

The book of Genesis tells us that after creating man and woman in his image "*God blessed them*," invited them to be fruitful and dominate the earth, and then: "*God saw everything that he had made, and behold, it was very good*" (Gen 1:28–31). This primal reality has not changed. God's gifts and calls are irrevocable, and even though sin complicated the situation, God has never taken back the blessing of life that he conferred on humankind. He cursed the serpent, but not the existence of humans. Existence is menaced by sin—we must be perfectly clear about that—but it remains essentially good; and the wound of sin quickly brings the promise of redemption through the still greater blessing prepared in Christ.

Grace does not change nature, it perfects it. How can we welcome the grace of redemption unless we welcome the gift of creation?Redemption restores and perfects the work of creation. It does not negate it or replace it.[1]

All this is more than a nice theory. It has very concrete consequences for our spiritual lives as individuals. Often, for example, I have observed in my ministry that what prevents some people from welcoming the grace

[1] The theme of fall and redemption is well developed in Christian thought, but creation may be insufficiently developed.

of God and paralyzes their human and spiritual progress is that they do not accept themselves as they are. They do not consent to their limitations as creatures.[2]

Creation, the act by which God calls us into being from nothingness, is his first great gesture of love and mercy in our lives. All God's other loving deeds toward us are grounded in this.

St. Catherine of Siena rhapsodizes on the beauty of the human person, created in the image of the Trinity. In the tradition of St. Augustine, she draws a connection between the three powers of the human soul—memory, intelligence, and will—and the members of the Trinity, and sees in creation a marvelous work of love.

O Deity, Deity, ineffable Deity! Supreme Goodness who by love alone has made us in your image and resemblance, you did not content yourself by saying, when you created Man, the "*Be made!*" that brought the other creatures out of nothingness; rather you said: "*Let us make Man in our image and resemblance*" (Gen 1:26), so that the entire Trinity combined in our existence and printed its form on the powers of our soul. And, in effect, O Eternal Father, in Whom all is preserved, our memory resembles You, because it retains and conserves all that our intelligence sees and understands of Yourself. This knowledge makes

---

[2] See the chapter on acceptance of self in my book *Interior Freedom.*

it participate in the wisdom of your only Son. You have also given the will of the Holy Spirit that abounds with Your love and seizes all that intelligence knows of Your ineffable goodness, to fill our memory and heart with You. Oh! Yes, I give You thanks for this infinite love that You manifested to the world, in giving us the intelligence to know You, the memory to retain You, the will to love You through all these things, as you deserve it; and this power, this love, neither the demon nor any creature can take from us without Your consent. How mankind should blush to see himself so loved and not love his Creator, his true life.[3]

In a wonderful catechetical discourse of January 2, 1980, John Paul II said: "The Creator is he who calls us to existence out of nothing, establishing the world in existence, and man in the world, because he is love." The Pope adds that this act signifies a fundamental spirit of giving. Directed to mankind, it establishes a relationship between the one who gives and the one who receives. "Creation is a gift, because mankind appears in it and, as the image of God, is capable of *understanding the very sense of the gift in the call to existence out of nothingness.*" These words shed light upon that intimate relationship between gift and call, evoked

[3] Catherine of Siena, *Prayers*. This prayer was made at Avignon for the re-establishment of peace in the Church.

above. "The call to existence out of nothingness" is not a metaphor; "call" here should be understood in its strongest sense, as vocation.

Furthermore, the fact that man and woman stand at the summit of creation is a sign that the call to life is a call to love, a call to encounter, a call to mutual self-giving. John Paul II said: "Mankind does not realize his essence except by existing with someone, and even more profoundly and more completely, by existing for someone." The body's sexual character signifies that the vocation to live is a vocation to interpersonal love and reciprocal giving.

Even before the gift of baptism and the particular callings that can follow from it—to marriage, to the consecrated life, to some apostolate or ministry—just to be a creature of God is already a great and beautiful vocation. It is a call to give thanks to God for the gift of life, to welcome life in its different aspects—corporal, intellectual, emotional, spiritual—and to orient us toward goodness and fruitfulness, particularly by mutual giving.

Unless aware of the beauty of our vocation as created beings, how can we welcome subsequent calls? What other basis do we have for dialogue with those who have not been baptized? The vocation to live is a vocation common to all humans, believers or not.

Every authentic vocation is a calling to live ever more fully. We should be wary of callings that may mask refusal to engage life, fear of love, flight from the body or feelings, or a lack of acceptance of human existence as it is. Accepting one's calling should mean choosing a more intense, abundant way of life, not fear-driving flight, or a disguised choice of death, as can happen with some poorly discerned religious commitments.

I WANT YOU TO LIVE

The sixteenth chapter of Ezekiel beautifully expresses the calling to live. The allegory sums up the history of Jerusalem, represented by a lovely young girl. She experiences betrayal and sin, but all ends well: God pardons her and restores her. First come the abandonment and rejection that everyone feels at some point in life:

> As for your birth, on the day you were born your navel string was not cut, nor were you washed with water to cleanse you, nor rubbed with salt, nor swathed with bands. No eye pitied you, to do any of these things to you out of compassion for you; but you were cast out on the open field, for you were abhorred, on the day that you were born (Ezek 16:4–5).

But fortunately, God passed and had pity:

> And when I passed by and saw you weltering in your blood. I said to you: Live! . . . You grew and developed,

you came to the age of puberty; your breasts were formed, your hair had grown . . . You were exceedingly beautiful, with the dignity of a queen (Ezek 16:6–13).

Live! I want you to live! Here is the first and the most fundamental call to us from God. When life seems too hard to bear we must hold tight to this word, will to respond to the call, choose to live and welcome life as it is, with all its burdens and sorrows. In the end, this confident acceptance will bring us to see life as an immense gift.

Many people have made this choice to believe in life despite their suffering. I think of Etty Hillesum, a young Jewish woman who died at Auschwitz in 1943 (I speak of her in my book *Interior Freedom*). "I am ready to testify, through all situations and even unto death, to the beauty and meaning of this life," she wrote.[4] The more humanly desperate the situation grew as a result of the Nazi persecution of Dutch Jews, the more confident of life she became.

Note that this means accepting life in its totality, not picking and choosing, accepting what pleases us and rejecting what doesn't. We must "choose all," as St. Thérèse of Lisieux said.[5] Etty Hillesum expressed the same thoughts:

---

[4] Etty Hillesum, *Une vie bouleversée* (Seuil), 166.

[5] St. Thérèse of Lisieux, *Complete Works*, Manuscript A, 9 and 10 (Cerf), 84.

I am having an ever-stronger experience these last days: in my least daily actions and sensations a hint of eternity creeps in. I am not the only one who is tired, sick, sad, or anguished. I am united with millions of others across centuries. All that is what life is made of. Life is beautiful and full of meaning in its absurdity if you know how to take it as a whole. So life in some sense or other forms a perfect whole. As soon as we refuse or wish to eliminate certain elements, as soon as we follow our own pleasure or caprice by accepting one aspect of life and rejecting another, then life becomes in effect absurd. Once the sense of the whole of it is lost, everything becomes arbitrary.[6]

Some time ago, after preaching on hope during a night of prayer in one of my community's houses, I had several minutes of conversation with an old lady that moved me deeply. She was over eighty, but beautiful, dignified, with a peaceful face. She told me she had encountered many trials in her life. In particular, when she was about thirty-five and had four children, her husband cruelly left her for another woman. For several weeks she was devastated, enclosed in her sadness and unwilling to live.

One day she heard an interior voice like that of Jesus: "If you do not lift yourself up, your children will

---

[6] Cited in Paul Lebeau, *Etty Hillesum, un itinéraire spiritual* (Albin Michel), 179.

not grow and mature." "I found the courage to go on," she told me, "to begin to live again and to take care of my children. It was not easy, I had many struggles, but the Lord was faithful and never abandoned me." She concluded: "Truly, life isn't what we think it is when we're twenty! But at the end of the day, it is full of marvelous gifts. . . . The secret is to consent to everything it puts before us!"

THE VALUE OF ALL OF LIFE

To a disturbing extent, contemporary Western culture has largely lost sight of these truths. It has difficulty recognizing the real value of every life, supposing instead that life is only worth living if one is rich, young, healthy, successful in everything, a potential subject of a fashion magazine cover. Handicap, old age, and suffering rob life of value. Yet fortunately the Church, faithful to the Gospel, ceaselessly proclaims the value of all life, even those lives that do not conform to society's current idea of success.

Remarkable testimonies exist capable of enlarging our hearts and our understanding. I think of one by Henri Nouwen, an acclaimed spiritual writer, who spent time in Jean Vanier's L'Arche community and found this contact with the handicapped an extraordinary source of conversion and enrichment. In one of his books, Nouwen writes movingly about Adam, a severely handicapped man who could not speak and was totally dependent on his friends for the needs of daily life, yet was an immense gift to others because of the peace that emanated from him and a presence that turned thoughts to what is essential.[7]

SIN IS A REFUSAL TO LIVE

Let us ask God to help us discern and undo our refusals to live. Sin somehow is always such a refusal, though it takes many forms: lack of hope, attachment to cramped projects, rejection of suffering, turning away from God and others, failure of confidence in the unique grace that accompanies our existence. Let us love and accept our lives—not imaginary lives—but the ones God offers us day by day, uncovering hidden riches for us as he does.

Up to now we have been considering the idea of calling. Now I turn to the chief ways that calls come to us, beginning with Holy Scripture.

[7] Henri Nouwen, *Adam, God's Beloved* (Orbis, 1997).

·· 3 ··

THE WORD OF GOD
AND ITS POWER TO CALL

It suffices for me to run my eyes over the Holy Scripture, and right away I breathe the perfumes of Jesus' life, and I know where to run.

—*Thérèse of Lisieux*[1]

God's Word, transmitted by Holy Scripture, is a fundamental means by which he calls us and communicates the gift of his life. Living with Scripture is not a luxury reserved for a few people of leisure or those with a taste for biblical exegesis. It is a vital necessity for every Christian, especially in these times of instability, struggle, and confusion. We have an urgent need for Holy Scripture as an inexhaustible source of light and strength, illumination and foundation of our lives. Jesus tells us: "*Heaven and earth will pass away, but my words will not pass away*" (Lk 21:33).

---

[1] St. Thérèse of Lisieux, *Complete Works*, Manuscript C, 36 verso, p. 285.

Scripture has a remarkable power to speak profoundly and personally to us, to respond to the exact here-and-now need for light, encouragement, and even conversion lodged deep in our hearts. Those moments when a Scripture verse, until then not especially meaningful, suddenly blazes out with a message that corresponds to our present situation testify to the faithfulness and tenderness of the Lord.

Let me begin with a beautiful text from the Second Vatican Council's dogmatic constitution on divine revelation, *Dei Verbum*. One of the unfortunate consequences of the Catholic reaction to excesses of the Protestant Reformation was a certain neglect of the Bible by ordinary Catholics. Vatican II sought to correct this—and spiritual movements like the Charismatic Renewal that have emerged since the Council are characterized by a great thirst for the Word of God. But let the Council fathers speak for themselves:

> The Church has always venerated the divine Scriptures, as she venerated the Body of the Lord, insofar as she never ceases, particularly in the sacred liturgy, to partake of the bread of life and to offer it to the faithful from the one table of the Word of God and the Body of Christ. She has always regarded, and continues to regard the Scriptures, taken together with Sacred Tradition, as the supreme rule of her faith. . . . It follows that all the preaching of the Church, as

indeed the entire Christian religion, should be nourished and ruled by Holy Scripture.[2]

The Council here speaks of Scripture as food for the faithful, much like the Eucharist. As St. Jerome said, *"We eat the body and drink the blood of Christ in the Eucharist, but also in listening to the Scriptures."*[3]

Note, too, the other expressions used to describe the Word as a precious gift from the Father: strength of our faith, nourishment of our soul, pure and permanent source of our spiritual life.

John Paul II took up this cue from Vatican II. To cite just one text, consider this from *Novo Millennio Ineunte*, which he addressed to the entire Church at the start of the third millennium:

It is especially necessary that listening to the Word of God become a life-giving encounter, in the ancient and ever valid tradition of *lectio divina*, which draws from the biblical text the living word which questions, directs, and shapes our lives.[4]

[2] *Dei Verbum*, in *Documents of Vatican II*, ed. A. Flannery (Grand Rapids: Eerdmans Publishing, 1975), no. 21.

[3] Cited by Enzo Bianchi, *Prier la Parole*, p. 30.

[4] Apostolic Letter *Novo Millennio Ineunte* of His Holiness Pope John Paul II to the bishops, clergy, and lay faithful at the close of the Great Jubilee of the year 2000, no. 39.

SCRIPTURE INVITES US TO READ SCRIPTURE

Scripture itself contains many invitations to meditate on God's Word. For example, Psalm 1: "*Blessed is the man who walks not in the counsel of the wicked . . . but his delight is in the law of the Lord, and on his law he meditates day and night.*" The psalm promises wonderful things to those who engage in this continual meditation: "*He is like a tree planted by streams of water, that yields its fruit in its season, and its leaf does not wither. In all that he does, he prospers.*"

And I love to cite this passage from the First Letter of Peter:

> Having purified your souls by your obedience to the truth for a sincere love of the brethren, love one another earnestly from the heart.
>
> You have been born anew, not of perishable seed but of imperishable, through the living and abiding Word of God; for: "All flesh is like grass and all its glory like the flower of grass. The grass withers, and the flower falls, but the word of the Lord abides for ever." That word is the good news, which was preached to you. Put away all malice and all guile and insincerity and envy and all slander. Like newborn babes, long for the pure spiritual milk, that by it you may grow up to salvation; for you have tasted the kindness of the Lord (1 Peter 1:22–2:3).

This moving passage invokes the power of the Word to engender in mankind a new life of health and love. It invites us to long for the Word as an infant craves its mother's milk, the food it must have to live and grow. It links listening to the Word with God's bounty, citing Psalm 34: "*Taste and see the goodness of the Lord!*" The experience of the divine bounty fills us with confidence and melts the hardness of our hearts. Reading Scripture can sometimes seem arid, but if we persevere, sooner or later we will find in it a sweetness more delicious than anything on earth.

GOD DWELLS IN HIS WORD

Scripture mysteriously communicates God's very presence. "My character, I give it in the text," the Talmud says, in a *midrash* or commentary on the Decalogue. Despite the limitations of the human languages used by biblical authors, the Holy Spirit who guided them made their words means by which God is truly among us in all his love, wisdom, and power.

Jewish and Christian traditions both testify to this. One should not exaggerate. But it would be a great mistake to think of the Bible as an ordinary book. When read in faith, it makes God himself present in our lives and communicates him to our hearts. If we allow the words of Scripture to fill our thoughts and enter our hearts, God becomes present. For God dwells in his Word.

It is often very different with us. Rarely do our words fully express our true selves, and often enough what we say is superficial, even untrue. When I say, "I love you" to someone, the words may carry the full weight of my freedom, my commitment, my faithfulness; or they may be a lie meaning only "I want something from you just now." But God is truth, and when he communicates, he communicates himself. Receiving his Word in our hearts means receiving the presence of God and his love and plunges us into intimacy with God.

The exchange of words between couples creates intimacy, a space for communication, for mutual giving, sometimes even for physical love. In the same way, listening to the Word and responding in prayer creates intimacy between God and the believer. This is fundamental, particularly for those committed to celibacy for the Kingdom. Time spent in *lectio divina* creates and deepens loving intimacy with God, without which the consecrated life loses all meaning. The fervent practice of *lectio divina* is absolutely necessary to live this way of life. It makes the consecrated person a spouse of the Word.

Meditation on Scripture is the foundation of any authentic Christian prayer life. God speaks to us and awakens a response from us through meditation. Here is how dialogue in prayer begins.

We need to find words to speak to God. Those that come to us spontaneously have their value of course, but Scripture suggests expressions and language for addressing God and in doing so helps shape our prayer. The Psalms, for example, are a beautiful gift in this way. They are human yet deeply spiritual, and express a vast range of sentiments—distress, anguish, the temptation to rebel, but also peaceful confidence and exultant joy. They always finish by making us confident and by inciting thanksgiving.

The more prayer is nourished by Scripture, the more it will be authentic and fruitful, at once fully human and yet capable of placing us in communion with the incomprehensible divine mystery. With Scripture in one's memory and heart, it becomes possible to respond to the mandate to "*Pray constantly!*" (1 Thess 5:17).

WORD AND DISCERNMENT

"*Thy word is a lamp to my feet,*" says Psalm 118. God's Word introduces the most profound light of truth into our lives. The letter to the Hebrews speaks of its power of discernment:

> For the Word of God is living and active, sharper than any two-edged sword, piercing to the division of soul and spirit, of joints and marrow, and discerning the thoughts and intentions of the heart. And before him no creature is hidden, but all are open and laid bare to the eyes of him with whom we have to do (Heb 4:12–13).

God's Word is something like a mirror by which we can truly know ourselves, good as well as bad. It passes judgment on our compromises with sin, our attempts to have it both ways and say yes as well as no, but it also highlights and encourages what is best in us. It enables us to discern between psychological constructs rooted in wounded humanity and outpourings of genuine love. Using this mirror metaphor, St. James invites us to apply ourselves to the Word, the "*perfect law of freedom*," so as to become attached to it and find happiness in living by it (Jas 1:25).

Assiduous reading of the Word provokes a beneficent crisis, a "judgment" (*krisis* in Greek—a term often encountered in the Gospel of John), which does not condemn but leads to conversion and salvation. I think, for example, of the parable of the owner of the vineyard who paid all his workers the same, those who worked only one hour and those who withstood the heat of the day, provoking angry grumbling from the latter (Mt 20:1–16). I think of these words:

> But I say to you, do not resist one who is evil. But if any one strikes you on the right cheek, turn to him the other also; and if any one would sue you and take your coat, let him have your cloak as well; and if any one forces you to go one mile, go with him two miles (Mt 5:39–41).

We are shocked by texts like these, but the shock is salutary. It brings to light human calculations, fears, and defense mechanisms. We are called to undertake self-improvement, to open ourselves to the work of grace, to have such confidence of God that we no longer need to calculate or be on guard, but can be capable of love in all circumstances. Thus God's Word draws us little by little from our human wisdom to the Wisdom of God.

LISTENING TO THE WORD, THE CONDITION FOR FRUITFULNESS IN OUR LIVES

One of the best-known parables of the Gospels speaks of the Word under the image of seeds that are sown.[5] In part, it warns against things that can make God's Word sterile in our lives—lack of perseverance, anxiety, riches, and pleasure. But the parable's first lesson concerns the fruitfulness of the Word. When "*understood with a noble and generous heart, that retains it and bears fruit by its steadfastness,*" it multiplies a hundredfold. The prophet Isaiah testifies to the same fruitfulness:

> For as the rain and the snow come down from heaven, and return not thither but water the earth, making it bring forth and sprout, giving seed to the sower and

[5]It is found in each of the synoptic Gospels: Mt 13:1–9; Mk 4:1-9, and Lk 8:4–15.

bread to the eater, so shall my word be that goes forth from my mouth; it shall not return to me empty, but it shall accomplish that which I purpose, and prosper in the thing for which I sent it (Isa 55:10–11).

Church history abounds with the witness of men and women who were touched and moved by a Word of God, and found meaning and fruitfulness in living by it. St. Anthony of the Desert (251–c. 356), father of all monks, was an Egyptian peasant who was swept off his feet at hearing these words read in his village church: "*If you wish to be perfect, go, sell what you have and give to the poor, and you will have treasure in heaven. Then come, follow me*" (Mt 19:21). The fruitfulness of his life and the immense success of the monastic lifestyle he inaugurated in the Church came from hearing the words and putting them into practice. Think, too, of Mother Teresa, who was moved to consecrate her life to serving the poor by Jesus' words: "*I am thirsty!*" As Pope John Paul II's 1996 encyclical letter, *Vita Consecrata*[6] says of the consecrated person that he or she "achieves spiritual fruitfulness in accepting the Word" as Mary did,[7] so also this is true for all Christians.

The vocation of each man or woman is in a certain sense to give flesh to the Word. The Word of God must be incarnated, to take flesh, or else it remains abstract

[6] Encyclical letter of John Paul II on consecrated life published in 1996.

[7] *Vita Consecrata*, no. 34.

and remote. At the same time, human life must be impregnated by God's Word, lest it be turned in on itself and lack eternal significance. There is no more beautiful thing in the world than a human heart that opens itself to the Word, perseveres in its desire to live that word to the end, and so is profoundly transformed and renewed. This is the very mystery of the Virgin Mary and the unimaginable fruitfulness of her life: "*Behold, I am the handmaid of the Lord. May it be done to me according to your word!*" (Lk 1:38).

As the Bible and the history of the Church make clear, the Word of God and the calls it transmits have power to awaken in our hearts treasures of generosity, love, and courage that can seem more than merely human. Self-giving gushes forth in ways surprising even to the beneficiary.

Consider the call of Levi, the future St. Matthew. He was a publican, one who collaborated with the Roman occupiers by collecting taxes and no doubt pocketing a good part of what was collected for himself. Needless to say, publicans were not held in high esteem. Jesus approached Levi as he sat engaged in his pestilent profession. He called him: "*Follow me!*" And Levi simply rose up and followed him (Mt. 9:9).

Later Levi (now Matthew, the disciple of Jesus) gave a great feast. Jesus was there, and so were Matthew's old friends—publicans, sinners, and women of evil life. The Pharisees were scandalized. And all except Jesus were astonished at the sudden change in the former tax collector. A man whose only concern had been to get rich, even by contemptible methods, becomes the disciple of an itinerant rabbi preaching the Kingdom of God! That doesn't happen everyday. Most surprised is Levi (Matthew) himself. Having welcomed the calling addressed to him, he felt something totally new emerge in him: courage to change, to enter upon a new adventure, to stop trying to be master of his own life and entrust himself to Another.

Levi could have found many reasons for saying to Jesus, "Call somebody else—some honest, practicing Jew. Think of my occupation. I'm not worthy." But Levi was mad enough—or wise enough—to welcome his unforeseen call. In doing that, he experienced how the Word that summoned him could also kindle in him a previously unimagined generosity, freedom, and disinterestedness. This is what Jesus meant when he declared: "*He who believes in me, as the scripture has said, 'Out of his heart shall flow rivers of living water*'" (Jn 7:38).

WORD OF GOD AND SPIRITUAL COMBAT: A WORD OF AUTHORITY

In chapter six of the Letter to the Ephesians, Paul exhorts his audience to take up with confidence and courage the combat that is an integral part of any authentically Christian life.

> Finally, be strong in the Lord and in the strength of
> his might. Put on the whole armor of God, that you
> may be able to stand against the wiles of the devil
> (Eph 6:10–11).

A little later, Paul describes the various components
of this armor that is needed to "*withstand in the evil
day, and having done all, to stand.*" The last, and not the
least, is "*the sword of the Spirit, which is the Word of God*"
(Eph 6:17).

This is an invitation to be more aware of Holy
Scripture as an indispensable aid in the trials of this life.
It is not simply human forces we face, but also, in a mys-
terious manner, realities of a spiritual order:

> For we are not contending against flesh and blood,
> but against the principalities, against the powers,
> against the world rulers of this present darkness,
> against the spiritual hosts of wickedness in the heav-
> enly places (Eph 6:12).

In his encyclical *Novo Millennio Ineunte*, laying out
his plan for the Church of the third millennium, Pope
John Paul says that a Christian who does not pray is a
Christian "at risk."[8] As a corollary, I'd add that the same
is true of a Christian who does not regularly read the

[8] *Novo Millennio Ineunte*, no. 34.

Word of God. It is a matter of life or death: "*Not by bread alone does man live, but by every word that comes forth from the mouth of the Lord*" (Deut 8:3). The world is too confused, and we are too weak, for us to try to live without the light and strength that come from the Bible.

The synoptic Gospels, especially Mark's, indicate how impressed the crowds were by the authority of Jesus' words: "*The people were astonished at his teaching, for he taught them as one having authority and not as the scribes*" (Mk 1:22). And again: "'*What is this? A new teaching with authority. He commands even the unclean spirits and they obey him*" (Mk 1:27). This authority means that Jesus spoke in his own name, not someone else's. This contrasts with the teaching of the rabbis of that time, who affirmed nothing without referring to the sages who came before—while of course adding a bit of their own. Jesus is not one more link in the transmission of the word. He is the Word itself.

Jesus' word is his power and effectiveness. When he casts out a demon, it flees without resisting. When he commands the stormy sea, "*Silence! Calm yourself!*" he produces great calm—not only for the boats, but also in the agitated hearts of the disciples. When he says to a poor sinner, "*Your sins are forgiven!*" the person immediately feels purified and reconciled with God and with himself, clothed in a new dignity, happy to be as he is.

There are moments in the lives of us all when the beneficent authority of God's Word will be our saving support, times of tribulation where the only stability will be found in the word of Scripture. Tempted in the desert by the Devil, Jesus overcame him with Scripture. But the Tempter will be stronger than we if we remain enclosed in human reasoning. Only the Word of God will have the ability to disarm him.

This holds true for all our experiences of trouble, doubt, and trial. Trying to find the way out by ourselves, we meet a dead end. The only way to achieve confidence, hope, and peace is by turning to Scripture. "*Do not worry about tomorrow*" (Mt 6:34). "*Fear not, little flock, for it is your Father's good pleasure to give you the kingdom.*" (Lk 12:32). "*Even the hairs of your head have all been numbered*" (Lk 12:7).

True peace comes in holding fast to the promises of God. When, in a moment of doubt or confusion, we accept a word of Scripture by an act of faith, the authority that belongs to this word becomes our support and strength. It is not a magic wand, immunizing us against perplexity and anguish. But it possesses a unique power, unlike anything else, to bring us hope no matter what happens. Accepted with faith, God's Word has the power to put an end to the ebb and flow of our uncertain reasonings, to establish us in truth and peace, to confer upon us the hope that is "*an anchor of the soul, sure and firm*" (Heb 6:19).

There are countless examples of Scripture that can be a precious resource in our struggles. If I feel alone and abandoned, Scripture demands: "*Can a woman forget her sucking child, that she should have no compassion on the son of her womb? Even these may forget, yet I will not forget you*" (Isa 49:15). If I feel that God is absent, it reassures me: "*I am with you always, until the end of the age*" (Mt 28:20). If I feel crushed by my sin, it tells me: "*Your sins I remember no more!*" (Isa 43:25). If I feel I lack what it takes to make progress, the Psalms invite me to make this act of faith: "*The Lord is my shepherd; I shall not want*" (Ps 23:1).

Not a day should pass for us without spending at least a few minutes reading Scripture. It may seem pointless at times, but if we persevere with simplicity and prayer, Scripture will enter deeply into our memories, without our even being aware. And when we need it, in a difficult moment, a verse will rise to consciousness. And it will be exactly the word that brings hope and peace.

THE WORD THAT NOURISHES FAITH, HOPE, AND LOVE

In the First Letter to the Thessalonians, Paul says: "*Let us be sober, and put on the breastplate of faith and love, and for a helmet the hope of salvation*" (1 Thess 5:8). The three theological virtues—faith, hope, and love—are our essential armament for any spiritual combat.

In any moment of trial they are likely to be challenged: What have you put your faith in? Where have you placed your hope, in God or in yourself? Is your love unconditional? Yet, every trial also is a call to make acts of faith and hope and to love more purely.

Holy Scripture possesses singular ability to encourage faith, fortify hope, and nourish love. St. Paul offers this wonderful thought in the Letter to the Romans:

> For whatever was written in former days was written for our instruction, that by steadfastness and by the encouragement of the scriptures we might have hope (Rom 15:4).

But the most significant passage of all is the story of the disciples at Emmaus. They had left Jerusalem with somber faces and heavy hearts, feeling that their hope in Jesus was crushed. Then suddenly a stranger joins them and explains the Scriptures. At the end, having recognized the Lord when he broke bread before disappearing from them, they hastened back to Jerusalem, renewed in faith and hope, to announce their encounter with the Risen Lord to the other disciples. And as they went they said to each other:

> Were not our hearts burning (within us) while he spoke to us on the way and opened the scriptures to us? (Lk 24:32).

When the Holy Spirit gives us wisdom to understand the Word, faith, hope, and love blaze up in our hearts.

THE WORD THAT HEALS AND PURIFIES THE HEART

To become familiar with Scripture, to have it penetrate our hearts and memories, brings profound healing over time. It isn't magic. Reading the Bible certainly doesn't replace competent professional therapy when that is needed. Yet, the Word of God does have healing power, as the spiritual experience of the desert monks and nuns in the early centuries of the Church attests. They sought personal conversion, purity of heart, and an encounter with God in continual prayer. One favorite means was Scripture, on which they sought to meditate and by which they attempted to live day and night. As a result, they achieved a piercing insight into the hidden compromises with evil and a purifying, authentic restructuring of the psyche leading to peace, freedom, and the fullness of their humanity.[9]

[9]See the description of Anthony by his biographer, St. Athanasius of Alexandria, as he was at the moment of his first contact with the faithful after years spent in solitude: "His aspect had remained the same, he was neither fattened by lack of physical exercise, nor emaciated by fasts and struggles against demons, but was as we knew him before his retreat. Spiritually pure, he was neither stricken by sorrow, nor dissipated by pleasure, in him there was no laugh nor sadness; the multitude of people did not trouble him, but neither did so many people greeting him give him excessive joy: always his same old self, governed by reason, natural. . . . His soul was in peace, his exterior senses were also untroubled; and yet, the joy of his soul gave him a joyful face; his body's movements betrayed his feeling and gave one an idea of the state of his heart, according to the word of the Scripture: a joyful heart makes a serene face. . . . This is how we perceived Anthony: he was never troubled, his soul was serene; never was he somber, his spirit was immersed in joy."

Our lives mirror the words that live in us. Memory, both conscious and unconscious, is like a reservoir of words, leading us to fashion our identities and conduct ourselves in certain ways. The dialogue that we carry on within us shapes our relationships with the world, with those close to us, and with ourselves. Some words were spoken to us as small children, and became imprinted in us. Some are beliefs we have derived from our experience of life, products of our education and cultural milieu. Some are bits and pieces carried on the continual tide of social life and media. These, too, can become convictions (*"This is how . . ."*), requirements (*"You must . . ."*), prohibitions (*"You must not . . ."*). Usually they do us little good, and often they box us in and immobilize us: *"I'll never get there," "I can't do it," "Life's a bitch," "No one understands me."* And so we are cut off from ourselves and reality, trapped in distorted relationships.

Scripture liberates. Little by little, the Word of God himself begins to live within us. Ceaseless meditation on Scripture draws the poison from the deadening words in our hearts, replacing them with words of confidence and encouragement: *"I can do all things in him who strengthens me"* (Phil 4:13), *"For with God nothing will be impossible"* (Lk 1:37), *"You are my beloved Son"* (Mk 1:11). Here are words of hope, truth, and love that purge the evil thoughts staining and darkening our hearts.

When read and understood with the guidance of the Holy Spirit, the Word of God is characteristically a word of encouragement, even when it forcefully denounces sin. To read it is not a bland exercise. It can jolt us like an earthquake and challenge our compromises with sin. But conversion and salvation, not condemnation, are its aim. When uncovering sin, it tells us that pardon is possible and God will accompany us and sustain us on our way. The liberation effected by the Word of God is a long process requiring great patience, yet one through which the Lord can work miracles.

THE WORD AND IDENTITY

God's Word, transmitted by Scripture, helps us live as the children of God that we are. Discovering this profound identity is imperative, for otherwise we are in danger of adopting false identities unable to withstand the trials that inevitably lie ahead. God's Word, addressed to us by the Father, tells us who and what we truly are.

Two fundamental words constitute our identity. The first word, as we already have seen, is the Word of creation that drew us from nothingness into being— God's animating, tender, merciful word, "See, I want you to live!" Creation, however, is not just a past event. It is God's continuing action sustaining us in existence. If God were to stop loving us and thinking of us for even one second, we would return to nothing. We are recipients and interlocutors of this creative word all through our lives.

The second word is the one inscribed upon us at baptism. It extends and deepens the Word of creation by giving us a much fuller life—the life of grace, filial adoption in Christ, participation in the life of the Trinity.[10] We hear it in Scripture, especially on the occasion of Jesus' baptism: "*You are my beloved Son in whom I am well pleased*" (Mk 1:11). The same might be said of us in virtue of our own baptism by which we become children in the Son.

All God's Words support us and invite us fully to welcome the filial life given us in Christ. They contain a gift and a call: the gift of being God's children and the call to grow in openness to the gift by cultivating simplicity, confidence, resignation, acceptance of the divine will, and thanksgiving. The spiritual life is something like a memory game whose objective is to re-establish contact especially with the two grace-filled words that already dwell in us and constitute our identity, in order to make them living and fruitful.

All this has enormous importance today, when many people no longer know to what or to whom they owe their existence. Anguish and insecurity and a sense

[10] In a sense, we are already children of God as creatures. Baptism adds a whole new dimension to the relationship of filiation. On this, see the reflections of Xavier Lacroix in *Passeurs de vie, essai sur la paternité* (Bayard, 2004), 282ff.

of emptiness are the result. "Scientific," atheistic culture encourages one to imagine that existence is the product of blind determinism (evolution, the mindless interaction of genes, and so forth) or a more or less haphazard coming-together of a man and a woman who made love without any thought of the new life that might come into existence. Often enough, in fact, that new life is seen as a failure of contraception. (I know someone whose life began when a condom ruptured.) Psychologists speak of the "survivor's syndrome" visible in the angst of a child born into a family in which there were several abortions: "Why is it that I escaped and not the others?"

Add to that the impact of being told that earth is only a small planet near an unremarkable star, in a remote corner of one galaxy among billions, and that the difference between humans and animals is not as great as we once thought, and how can anyone feel loved and wanted?[11] The universe could get along without us. Humans are useless products of an impersonal cosmos. If contemporary secular culture makes anything clear, it is this: The rejection of God breeds self-disgust.

[11] I am not denying or denigrating the discoveries of modern science. What we know today about the universe, about evolution, and about genetics is fascinating and for believers a marvelous testimony to the wisdom and power of God. But in an atheistic context, interpreted and vulgarized in exclusively materialistic terms, these scientific truths can have a destructive impact on people's image of themselves and their understanding of life.

The only remedy for this wound to human consciousness is the sense of our filiation, the discovery of our divine parentage. Whatever the circumstances of my conception and birth, my existence itself means that I was wanted, chosen, and loved by an unimaginably tender, pure, unconditional, and generous lover: our creator God. How urgently we need to regain contact with our origins in the creative act of God![12]

The Word of God offers us this contact. Scripture gives us access to the word already mysteriously inscribed within us: "*I said to you: Live!*" (Ezek 16:6).

SOME PRACTICAL CONSIDERATIONS

Let me conclude this chapter on encountering God's Word as a special place of calling and spiritual growth with some practical considerations. (The book also includes as an appendix a simple method of *lectio divina*.)

For reading of Scripture to be fruitful, the following things are necessary:

1. The reading must be done in the context of prayer. Only the Holy Spirit can open to us the profound, living sense of Scripture. Humble, persevering, confident prayer is the basis of all exegesis.

---

[12] I sometimes wonder if one reason for the frenzy about sex in today's world is not this need to make contact with our origins.

2. We must have the mindset of faith, believing that God truly comes to speak personally with us through Scripture. It is not a matter of having great learning. Thérèse of Lisieux had made no advanced biblical studies (although, intrigued by differences in translation, she would have liked to learn Greek and Hebrew), but that did not prevent her from having a very profound wisdom concerning certain passages of the Bible—in which she found the spiritual intuitions that earned her the title of Doctor of the Church.

> The Gospels support me during my prayers, and I find all that is necessary for my poor little soul there. I always discover new insights and hidden and mysterious meanings in them.[13]

3. The third condition is a true desire for conversion—to want unreservedly that the Word disclose to us our sins so that we can love God and one another with more authentic love. This desire for conversion is the key to productive *lectio divina*. Reading the word is not a kind of spiritual sightseeing, not a way of learning biblical culture or acquiring homily material. It is meant to be a guide for living. This was the typical attitude of the Desert Fathers.

[13] St. Thérèse of Lisieux, *Complete Works*, Manuscript A, p. 83, reverse.

Someone went off to find abba Pambo, asking him to teach him a Psalm. Pambo began to teach Psalm 38, but he had hardly pronounced the first verse: "*I said: 'I will stay the route, without letting my language go astray,'*" then the brother no longer wanted to hear any more. He said to Pambo: "This verse suffices for me; would that it please God that I have the strength to learn it and to put it in practice." Nineteen years later, he was still striving to.[14]

Reading Scripture is taking a risk: that we will be asked to reorder our lives or told things we don't want to hear. We do not work on the Bible. It works on us.

Sometimes certain verses can hold us in their grip for weeks on end. Once, during a session of *lectio,* I was particularly struck by the words of St. Paul: "*For though I am free from all men, I have made myself a slave to all*" (1 Cor 9:19). I pondered that for many days. Was I truly free in regard to others? Emotionally free? Free from the pressure of opinions? Did I truly place myself at the service of my brothers and sisters in everyday life?

[14] Cited in a beautiful lesson on *lectio divina* by Cistercian Sister Marie Pascale. Available on the Internet: *http://users.skynet.be/scourmont/Armand/wri/lectio-fra.htm.*

4. Although it is important that Scripture speak to each of us personally, the reading of the Word of God should not become individualistic. What we think we have discovered there must be tested by the teaching of the Church and received in communion with all those who, with us, make up the body of Christ. The belief that a particular passage is a personal call to oneself, with important implications for one's life, requires confirmation by a spiritual guide. Interpretations that are overly literal or fundamentalist or ignore ecclesial communion are to be avoided. Any understanding of the Word should be reasonable—not narrowly rationalistic, but open to mystery, enlightened by faith, and in harmony with the thinking of the Church.

•• 4 ••

LIFE'S EVENTS

Lord, you speak personally to all men by what happens to them from moment to moment.[1]

Now let us turn to a second way in which God's calls can come to us. I mean the events of life. The Hebrew word *davar* has two meanings: word and event. Reasonably so, since the encounter with the Word of God, if authentic, is truly an event. Every event likewise is a word, and the light shed by Scripture often enables us to discern what God is telling us or calling us to through particular events.

Everything that happens to us is in some way or other a call from God—to grow, to change, to see things differently, and to undergo conversion.[2]

[1] *L'abandon à la providence divine,* formerly attributed to Jean-Pierre de Caussade (DDB, 2005), 137.

[2] This is true of everyone, not just believers. Life is a school for us all; a difficult and demanding school, but one full of wisdom. Some let themselves be educated with confidence and docility, and make rapid progress. Others rebel. Here is the mystery of human free will.

While many circumstances of our lives are not direct products of God's will, Scripture invites us to believe that God is present in everything and can bring what is good for us out of even the most difficult situations. The saints testify with total unanimity to this confidence in divine providence. But to bring goodness from everything, God seeks our cooperation. Whatever happens, even if it is the consequence of error or sin, can be received and understood as a call from God.

This truth is fundamental, but it should not lead us to attempt to interpret events in a superficially "spiritual" way reflecting fundamentalism or fatalism. Often we do not know the meaning of what happens. The calls God sends us through events must emerge gradually and be discerned with prudence, without imposing interpretations on them. Meanwhile, the essential thing is to welcome events and live them out with faith, even if we don't understand them.

Another danger to avoid is a scrupulous attitude, pressuring us to find the meaning of everything lest we violate God's will. This is a fear rooted in a psychological need for security that separates us from the simplicity and freedom of God's children.

Yes, there are subtleties and complexities here, but they should not obscure the fundamental point. Listening for God's calls makes it possible for us to live every situation positively and opens a pathway to freedom in every situation, even the most seemingly hopeless.[3]

HAPPY EVENTS, CALLS TO GRATITUDE AND GIVING

Everything that happens contains a call from God. The big and little happinesses of life are first and foremost calls to thanksgiving, and the happiness will be even greater if we respond. It is a joyful thing to receive a gift but even more joyful to give thanks for it.

Giving thanks is beautiful because it is just, because it deepens our relationship with the giver, and also because it expands one's heart, making it receptive to still more graces. St. Thérèse of Lisieux understood this, as a bit of advice recorded by her sister Céline makes clear:

> What most attracts God's grace is recognition, because if we thank him for a blessing, he is touched and he hastens to offer us ten other graces, and if we thank him with the same exuberance, what an incalculable multiplication of graces would ensue! I have seen this, try it and you will see! My gratitude is without limits for what he has given me, and I express it in a thousand ways.[4]

[3] A good definition of freedom is: the capacity to live each situation positively, not being enclosed or crushed, but of finding the way of belief and a more authentic life. This is the glorious freedom of the children of God that Christ acquired for us by his death and resurrection.

[4] Sister Geniviève of the Holy Face, *Advice and Memoirs* (Cerf).

God's gifts are also invitations to have confidence, to welcome life, to share, to make what we are given fruitful for others, and to accept responsibility. They summon us to give ourselves and exhibit the same generosity that we have been shown.

SORROWFUL EVENTS, CALLS TO GROW

Sorrowful events also contain calls, though with a different content. They can be invitations to faith, to hope, to patience, to courage, to acts of forgiveness, to acceptance of our limits . . . the list is endless. But there is always some particular point, and it does not necessarily become clear to us all at once.

When someone is in a difficult situation, the most important thing to do, and the most liberating, is not to resolve the situation—something often beyond the person's capacity—but to understand and follow the call present in the situation. It is not always readily discernible at first, but it will be revealed little by little to one who consents to the situation and sincerely asks what God wants of us.

When the Gospel says that Jesus is the way,[5] it speaks beautiful words of hope. There are no circumstances in which the living presence of Jesus, hidden though it may be, cannot guide us, remove the obstacles

---

[5] "I am the way, the truth, and the light" (Jn 14:6).

blocking us, give us the strength to move ahead each day. Psalm 16 says: *"You will show me the path to life, abounding joy in your presence, the delights at your right hand forever."*

But the Lord's assistance is no magic wand—an intervention that makes everything go better without our active cooperation. God acts for us, but never without us—never without inviting our intellects to see things in a new light and giving us freedom to choose as we ought. Every divine intervention in one's life comes with a call to conversion. "I created you without you," the Lord said to St. Catherine of Siena, "but I will not save you without you."

ASKING THE RIGHT QUESTIONS

We have many questions in troubled times: "How can I go on?" "How long will this last?" "Why is this happening to me?" "Who's to blame?" "Is it normal for this to happen?" These questions are fair enough, and sometimes answering them can even help us solve our problems.

But often there are no answers. One can spend a lifetime, for instance, trying to assign responsibility for a situation without succeeding. Instead of being bent on getting answers, one needs the courage to leave certain legitimate questions unanswered—something always painful—and adopt a different perspective: "At the end of the day, what does God want from me in all this?"[6]

Since we crave to understand everything, this calls for a kind of conversion. But it is worth the effort, for sooner or later there will be a response. Someone who sincerely seeks God's will can count on knowing it in the end. "He would sooner make stones speak than not manifest his will to his children who search it confidently," said Jean-Jacques Olier, founder of the Sulpicians.[7]

In the course of spiritual direction, I have often observed that people in difficult situations who come to terms with their inability to understand everything and begin to ask what God wants of them here and now receive enlightenment little by little. Perhaps an act of confidence is made, or forgiveness is accepted, or there is a renewed effort to pray. Relief and release are the result, and a pathway to the future opens up.

I remember something that happened several years ago. When I preach a retreat, people often come to see me for private conversations. This time a young woman told me: "Father, everything in my life is going wrong.

---

[6] It is good to remember a fundamental point: It is not knowledge that saves but faith. What saves (helps us advance and grow in a positive, fruitful manner) is not being able to explain everything or completely grasping the complexity of every situation or parceling out responsibility. It is finding the right attitude, the one to which God invites us. Faith lies in welcoming situations with confidence and submitting our conduct to the will of the Holy Spirit.

[7] Cited in B. Pitaud and G.. Chaillot, *Jean-Jacques Olier, Spiritual Doctor* (Cerf), 243.

It's a disaster!" Humanly speaking, she was not exaggerating. I listened to her attentively, for someone in pain must be truly listened to and his or her sorrow must be understood. Her fiancé had left her, she was out of work, she had family difficulties, a bad relationship with her father, etc. As I listened, I said to myself: "My God, how can I possibly help her?" But as she spoke, at least one thing became clear: first of all, she had to forgive her father. The Lord would have to take care of the rest. God's call was clear: "Forgive your father." We prayed together for a moment, she confessed her sins, and now she had the courage to decide to forgive and leave the rest to God.

The young woman left peaceful and content. She understood what she needed to do, she had become an agent in her life again, and she felt confidence in God and in herself. She might have said: "Everything is going well in my life!"

If people know what they must do today and commit themselves to doing it and leave tomorrow to God's providence, all is well. What more can anyone do? Take the step that needs taking today. Take another step tomorrow. Every day will have its own steps to take.

Things don't always happen so simply, of course, yet I find it deeply moving to observe God's graces of light and reconciliation at work in those who sincerely seek his help and guidance. Time and again I have seen change occurring in someone with whom I was speaking. First: "I have a problem and I've come to you for a solution." But the Holy Spirit takes a hand, and then: "What is God asking of me in all this?" Or: "Where are the most faith, hope, and love to be found?" These are questions that have answers—if not at least for today. And that is enough.

In problematic circumstances, progress lies in hearing the calls that are being addressed to us. *"Shema Israel, Listen, Israel!"* One must pass from "What do I want from life?" to "What does life want from me?" Or, sometimes from "What do I expect from those around me?" to "What do those around me expect of me?" Whatever words are used, this conversion is always necessary and always fruitful. The Gospel very often invites us to make this change of perspective.

> Whatever you wish that men would do to you, do so to them; for this is the law and the prophets (Mt 7:12).

TRUE AND FALSE RESPONSES

The answer to the question "What call is the situation addressing to me?" does not exist before the situation exists. It is not a ready-made response or a kind of psychological projection. It is similar to grace; it is like a gift. It comes in the opening of the heart and the beginning of prayer. Often one finds it in the encounter with the Word of God, and often it has the unexpected newness that is the mark of the Spirit. It gives peace and liberates.

Often one's pre-existing responses have little to do with God's true call. They reflect one's habitual way of thinking, the coping strategies one has grown accustomed to. At first they may seem very spiritual and edifying. But they are not the will of God. To hear the true call of the Spirit, one must know one's self and listen to others who often see things more clearly. Then we generally detect pretty quickly what comes from God and what comes from the "flesh," as Paul calls it—which might also be called the wounded psyche.

It may be one's habit to blame oneself for life's problems. Or to blame others. Or to think one must be heroic in a way that God doesn't ask. A person may have a fear of weakness, believing that he or she must always be strong. Some of us are in denial; some are always taking flight. These are paths that lead to rigidity, worry, and tension.

The responses that come from the Spirit are different. They are in harmony with the Word of God; they have the flavor of evangelical sweetness, of humility and peace, a note of simplicity and realism. They are also characterized by freshness and newness, and give rise to confidence. Although it sometimes takes courage to accept them, they are not restrictive in nature, not imposed from the outside, but are part of an interior dynamism that respects freedom. They lead us out of our repetitious scenarios and produce true changes. They produce a renewal in our lives that can only come from God.

The grace that St. Thérèse of Lisieux received at Christmas in 1886 is a powerful example.[8] She was fourteen then, and she could not have taken up her vocation to Carmel without it. Sometimes she speaks of it as a grace of conversion and sometimes a grace of healing.

At the time, Thérèse had an immense love of Jesus and a very authentic spiritual life, along with a great deal of emotional immaturity. She was hypersensitive, shed tears for no reason, exaggerated her need for the attention and approval of her family. After Midnight Mass it was time for the traditional opening of presents. Thérèse had gone upstairs to take off her hat. Her father, Mr. Martin, sleepy and no doubt tired of treating his youngest daughter as a child, expressed his weariness: "Well, fortunately it is the last year!" Everybody expected that Thérèse, hearing those words, would react as usual and burst into tears, ruining the occasion for the family.

But now the future saint perceived God's call: Leave the limitations of childhood, get the better of your feelings, come downstairs, as cheerful as if you'd heard nothing. She made up her mind to do that, and received a great healing: "I found again the strength of

---

[8] St. Thérèse of Lisieux, *Complete Works*, Manuscript A 45 r (Cerf), 142.

soul that I had lost at the age of four and a half." Now she could start on her giant's course toward sainthood, as she called it.

As with Thérèse, so with us: welcoming the calls of grace, even in small things, bears much fruit.

EVERY CALL IS A CALL TO BELIEVE, TO HOPE, AND TO LOVE

As we have seen, what God calls people to can be very different, depending on the unique paths he intends for them. They can be calls to patience, pardon, a concrete commitment to service, prayer, self-acceptance, abandonment to God's will, humility, an act of tenderness, the welcoming of a joyful event, and much else.

But, despite the vast diversity, the calls we receive are always in the end invitations to believe, hope, or love. These three "theological virtues" are a fundamental driving force of the spiritual life.

The order in which they are revealed to us is important. The first of God's calls in any situation—and especially in difficult ones—is a *call to faith*: to believe that God is present, is faithful, holds all things in his hand, and has not forgotten us. This most profound and radical call of our Father God is a call to confidence. Next comes the *call to hope*: to expect his help and not just help from ourselves, to place our trust in him and not in human striving.

On this basis of faith and hope, we then are open to God's *calls to love*: a truer, purer love of God, of neighbor, of oneself.

Faith and hope are the foundations of charity. And it is love in the end that will remain. "*If I . . . do not have love, I am nothing*" St. Paul says.[9] Contemplation will take the place of faith, hoping will be fulfilled in having. But nothing else will replace love. The experience of loving God and neighbor in the kingdom of heaven will be more ardent and pure than the experience of loving them now, but its substance will not change.

Every trial, no matter what it may be—a health problem, a professional setback, a spiritual crisis, hard times in a relationship, or anything else—is a test of faith. Do you believe that God is present in this experience? Do you still believe in his love and his promises? Do you believe in his fidelity, his strength, in the fact that he makes everything come together for your good?

Every trial is also a test of hope. For whose salvation are you looking—only your own? Do you expect it to come about from something you do? From other human means? Or essentially from God? In what or whom do you place your trust? Your money, your street smarts, your advanced degree, your virtues, some person or institution? Or have you placed your trust only in God, and his infinite mercy?

[9] 1 Cor 13:2.

Often, finally, trials are tests of love. This is especially true in relationships, notably including the conflict that couples experience. Is your love genuine? Is it disinterested? Does it have staying power? This apparent generosity of yours—is it real or is it only a disguised bargain (giving only as much as you get in return)?

We should not fear the trials in life. They are necessary and beneficial, provided we recognize in them the calls that God is sending us. This is how we grow. Trials hold out to us the gift of an increase in faith, confidence, and love. Recall Peter's wonderful words about faith:

> Blessed be the God and Father of our Lord Jesus Christ! By his great mercy we have been born anew to a living hope through the resurrection of Jesus Christ from the dead, and to an inheritance which is imperishable, undefiled, and unfading, kept in heaven for you, who by God's power are guarded through faith for a salvation ready to be revealed in the last time. In this you rejoice, though now for a little while you may have to suffer various trials, so that the genuineness of your faith, more precious than gold which though perishable is tested by fire, may redound to praise and glory and honor at the revelation of Jesus Christ (1 Pet 1: 3–7).

The apostle James even goes so far as to tell us: "*Consider it all joy, my brothers, when you encounter various trials*" (Jas 1:2).

THE THREE AXES OF LOVE

Now let us consider calls to love and the different forms they can take.

When Jesus was asked which was the greatest commandment, he replied:

> You shall love the Lord, your God, with all your heart, with all your soul, and with all your mind. This is the greatest and the first commandment. The second is like it: You shall love your neighbor as yourself. The whole law and the prophets depend on these two commandments (Mt 22:37–40).

Love travels along two paths that are inseparable in the end: love of God and love of neighbor. But as this text suggests, there is another aspect of charity—love of one's self. (*"You shall love your neighbor as yourself."*) This self-love is good and necessary, not egoism that refers everything to "me," but the grace to live in peace with one's self, consent to be what one is, with one's talents and limitations.

Love of God, love of neighbor, and love of self grow together and sustain one another as they grow. If one is absent or neglected, the other two suffer. Like the legs of a tripod, all three are needed in order to stand and each leans on the others. As there are six possible relationships among three entities, so there are six here.

1. Love for other people is supported by love of God. Without the strength we draw from it, patience, forgiveness, and mercy would be difficult. The capacity to love would diminish unless constantly renewed through prayer and sacraments in him who is love's source. Love is often stifled by discouragement or despair, and only healthy hope in God gives the courage needed to persevere in love.

2. Love toward others is also supported by love of self. If I do not accept myself as I am, it will eventually be reflected in resentment and conflict. Many conflicts with others are projections of conflicts with ourselves: I refuse to put up with the failings of others because I do not accept my own. If I am not at peace with myself, I make others pay for my unhappiness.

3. Love of God needs love of neighbor. If I close my heart to others and am hardened by narrow judgments, accusations, or grudges, I cannot experience the tenderness and bounty of God and grow in love of him. "*For the measure you give will be the measure you get back*" (Lk 6:38). So, for example, refusing to forgive someone can totally deaden one's spiritual life.

4. Love of neighbor also supports love of self. Those who close themselves off from love of others close themselves off from what is best about themselves.

They lose opportunities to be reconciled with themselves, an experience that often is mediated by others. If one is unbending and hard toward others, one's own misery will shortly be disclosed, whereas one's forgetfulness of self in order to love others leads to self-discovery. By the grace she received in the Christmas incident described above, St. Thérèse of the Child Jesus says: "I felt charity enter my heart, the need to forget myself in order to please, and since then I was happy!"[10]

5. Love of God also requires love of self. Not to accept myself as I am means not recognizing God's love for me. In loving me after all, God is not loving some ideal being, the person I "ought to be" or "would like to be." He takes me just as I am, and I cannot fully welcome this love without accepting myself. Pride, perfectionism, and fear of rejection are among the obstacles to that.

6. Finally, love of self is built up by love of God. Those who close themselves to God will sooner or later come to hate themselves. For the tenderness of the Father and his welcoming regard are the surest path to self-acceptance, whereas rejecting God leads to self-hatred. People today have great difficulty loving themselves—the proliferation of pop psychological books on personal development and

[10] St. Thérèse of Lisieux, *Complete Works* (Cerf), 143.

the acquisition of self-esteem are symptoms of that. Google "self-esteem" and the result is 1.4 million pages in French alone!

My message isn't "Back to the Middle Ages," but I'm convinced that people several centuries ago didn't find it as hard to love themselves as we do now. Those people of earlier times knew perfectly well that they were creatures of God—sinners, certainly, but worthy of love and redemption; capable of great mistakes, but eligible for salvation. The rejection of God over the last three centuries was accompanied by the illusion that guilt would be eliminated in this way and human beings would finally be free and happy. But those who thought like that forgot something: without God, humankind must carry on its own the weight of distress, misery, and failings of all kinds. If there is no God, there is no pardon or mercy. Whoever makes a botch of his life has no way of being forgiven. Not even an army of therapists can teach us to absolve ourselves. Self-esteem must be based on the certitude that, whatever happens, I am loved and I can love. And only God can guarantee that.

The core of one's personality, the ground of that intimate security everyone needs, resides upon the dual certainty of being loved and being able to love. Both are necessary. Knowing that one is loved unconditionally is not enough by itself; one needs also to know that one can love and make a disinterested gift of self—that one can be fruitful and give life. Only God can guarantee this double certainty: only he loves us with an entirely unconditional love and only he assures us that, despite our limits, his grace can create in our hearts a true aptitude for loving, for being able to receive and being eager to give.

Love of God, love of neighbor, and love of self develop together, but at any given time we may find it necessary to emphasize one more than the others. Sometimes it may be intensifying love of God by praying more, trusting him more, being more open to his will, listening more carefully to his word. Sometimes it will be loving one's neighbor—practicing patience (according to St. Catherine of Siena, "the model of charity"), extending forgiveness, serving others, helping the poor, and so on. And sometimes the priority has to be self-love: consenting to one's fragility and frailty, accepting oneself, ceasing to blame oneself. We must be attentive to the Spirit's calls and discern his priorities at each particular point in our lives.

ATTITUDES THAT MAKE US RECEPTIVE TO CALLING

But how do we discern God's calls? What form should faith, hope, and love take for me here and now? It is not always easy to say, and no one-size-fits-all formula suits everyone. But certain attitudes do shed light on the vast majority of the cases and help guide our decisions. It is not a matter of cultivating some refined technique of discernment, but living in the state of interior receptivity about which I shall speak later. Six related attitudes are indispensable, to this end.

1. The first is the attitude of prayer. "*Ask and you shall receive, knock and it shall be opened unto you.*"[11] "*Pray at all times in the Spirit, with all prayer and supplication. To that end keep alert with all perseverance, making supplication for all the saints.*"[12] Beyond being faithful to one's set times of prayer, one needs a great desire to live for God and to love him in all things—to be in his presence as much as possible in all circumstances of life in order to be in dialogue with him. Brother Lawrence of the Resurrection, a lay brother at the Carmelite monastery in Paris in the seventeenth century, wrote as follows:

> The most holy practice, the most ordinary and necessary for spiritual life in the presence of God, is to be pleased with and accustomed to divine company, to speak humbly and converse with him at all times, during each moment, without rules or measurement of time, especially in times of temptation, pain, spiritual dryness, and even moments of infidelity or sin. It is necessary to apply ourselves

[11] Lk 11:9.
[12] Eph 6:18.

continuously and indifferently to this, so that all of our actions become a sort of little interview with God, not as a studied effort, but coming from the purity and simplicity of the heart.[13]

2. A second fundamental attitude that we should have is the attitude of *faith*, with its two inseparable aspects: *confidence* and *obedience to the truth.* Total confidence in God means abandoning ourselves entirely to his care like little children, even in the worst storms (think of the calming of the tempest in the Gospel account).[14] At the same time, we must have a great desire to welcome the truth and submit to it, according St. Peter's beautiful prescription: "*Having purified your souls by your obedience to the truth for a sincere love of the brethren, love one another earnestly from the heart*" (1 Pt 1:22). St. Thérèse used to say: "I have never looked for anything but the truth."[15] Sincerity—always being truthful with oneself, with others, and with God—is a powerful engine of spiritual progress. This can be seen, for example, in the life of Etty Hillesum. Although her moral and emotional lives were not too well defined at the start, this young woman had an authentic devotion

[13] Conrad De Meester, O.C.D., Brother Lawrence of the Resurrection. *Writings and Interviews on the Practice and Presence of God* (Cerf, 1991).

[14] Mk 4:35–40.

[15] St. Thérèse of Lisieux, *Last Interviews*, 30 September.

75

to God and manifested admirable kindness toward others; as her journal shows, she craved and clung to the truth.[16]

One of the most authentic expressions of the desire for truth is *humility*: the ability to recognize one's errors, to allow oneself to be educated by others and by life, to escape the trap of always having to be right and getting to have the last word, which does so much harm to relationships and often gets in the way of truth.

Walking in faith also means *consenting to a kind of obscurity*, learning to live with questions we cannot answer. This clashes with our need for security and with the illusion that security lies in intellectual mastery of situations. But that is a mistake. We cannot understand everything, and recognizing our limits and placing our trust in God is the true road to security and peace.

I have often encountered people who've experienced painful emotional ruptures and have difficulty forgiving and getting on with their lives. They remain mired in their suffering, determined to understand everything that happened, to know why the other person thought as he or she did, to comprehend why they were "dumped." Sometimes our condition for turning the page is that everything be

[16] Etty Hillesum, *A Overturned Life* (Seuil, 1985).

made clear to use—and that can't happen. Then the only way to move ahead is by abandoning ourselves to God and his wisdom in showing us what he wishes to show when he wishes to show it. This letting-go is hard, but healthy.

3. Third comes *living in the present moment.* God doesn't always send long-term solutions in response to our needs but often only little boosts, "just for today."[17] That is enough for us to go on, provided we have confidence in God.

On this subject I greatly admire a passage from St. John of the Cross' poem *The Obscure Night*:

On that glad night,

In secret, for no one saw me,

Nor did I look at anything,

With no other light or guide

This guided me

More surely than the light of noon

Than the one that burned in my heart.[18]

Following the small flame of faith, hope, and love that burns in the heart, the soul feels as secure

[17] St. Thérèse of Lisieux, Poetry 5, *Complete Works* (Cerf/DDB), 645.
[18] Taken from the translation of Kieran Kavanaugh, OCD, and Otilio Rodriguez, OCD, in *The Collected Works of St. John of the Cross*, revised edition (1991).

as if it walked in broad daylight. Let us follow the indications arising from the humble acts of faith, hope, and love the Holy Spirit inspires us to make daily. We cannot go wrong in believing, hoping, and loving. God speaks today for today. We can't know what we will be called to do five or ten years from now. Knowing what we should do today is enough.

Someone with this attitude possesses flexibility and detachment. It is not good to want always to be in charge of one's life and to be rigid in scheduling as a result. To be sure, it's desirable to have an organized life and an orderly agenda, but only while remaining open to the unexpected. If we are too locked into our plans, we are in danger of missing God's calls.

During a retreat for priests at Medjugorje, the witness of a Spirit-filled sister struck me. Sister Elvira was foundress of a splendid facility for helping young drug addicts. She told us something we priests needed to hear: "I am always ready to do, in the next five minutes, just the opposite of what I had planned!"

4. Another indispensable attitude is that of consent to the situation in which we find ourselves, especially *consent to suffering.* This is not just passivity in putting up with whatever happens, and much less is it the active pursuit of suffering. Relieve the suffering that

can be relieved! Do not make a deity of suffering for its own sake. It is love that saves, not suffering.

Yet some suffering and struggle are part of every life. They must be borne with patience, in faith and hope, with the strength that one finds in Christ. Paul tells his disciple Timothy: "*Share in suffering for the Gospel in the power of God*" (2 Tim 1:8). St. Peter urges us not to consider times of trial something foreign: "*But rejoice in so far as you share Christ's sufferings, that you may also rejoice and be glad when his glory is revealed*" (1 Pet 4:13).

I do not wish to say a great deal about something I've discussed elsewhere,[19] but a few remarks may be in order here. Accepting suffering is always difficult, but it simplifies life, while the refusal to suffer complicates life enormously. In that case we are endlessly required to devise wearying, complex schemes for avoiding sorrow. Otherwise it feeds rancor, spurs rebellion, and leads to charges and countercharges that poison our hearts. It is not uncommon for people to turn simple situations into maddeningly complicated ones, just by refusing to suffer.

Christianity is often accused of being soft on suffering. But who is more suffering's friend in the end—the man who accepts difficulties with robust

[19] In my work *Interior Freedom* (Scepter Publishers, Inc., 2007).

faith or the one who spends his time moaning and groaning about the predictable problems of living?

The radical refusal of suffering pervading Western culture today has perverse effects. Those who suffer are encouraged to consider themselves sick people or victims. But this is ruinous for social relations. Christian writings about the redemptive value of suffering sometimes overdid that theme, but the present denial that suffering can have any positive meaning does far more harm.

Often suffering is treated as if it were a disease. To help and accompany someone who is grieving is one thing: to consider such an individual as being in an abnormal state and in need of psychological counseling is quite different. We appear desperate to heal everything. An ad in a Christian magazine read: "Cure your family wounds!" I don't doubt the good intentions of the organizers of a retreat for people who had been hurt by family troubles. But the slogan surprised me. Family life is not a sickness. Are we soon to see ads headed "Get over living"? The only way to get over life is to die! Behind an obsession with healing may be a refusal to live life as it is.

"Victimization" also is in these days. Since suffering is unacceptable, it must be unjust. So anyone who suffers must be a victim. This way of thinking fuels infantile demands and unrealistic reparations.

But I repeat: All the suffering that can be removed should be removed. The Gospel tells us to feed the hungry and clothe the naked. At the same time, though, we need to accept as much suffering as human and spiritual progress require. Suffering accepted liberates the psyche from the slough of egoism, reorienting it to spiritual vitality and self-giving. This suffering opens us to the mystery of God: "*Many are the afflictions of the righteous; but the Lord delivers him out of them all*" (Ps 34:19).

Consenting to suffering also brings peace—the peace that enables one to hear God's calls.

5. Another attitude necessary for discerning God's calls is willingness to be accompanied. No one is self-sufficient. As St. John of the Cross remarks, God wills that we need one another: "God is extremely pleased that people are governed and directed by other people similar to themselves."[20] How good it is to know that one can turn to someone else and speak candidly about what one is experiencing, in the confidence that this is a way of receiving God's light!

Merely to put into words what is happening is itself beneficial because it fosters objectivity and clarity. But especially beneficial is the humility involved in recognizing that one cannot understand the deepest reality of one's life entirely unaided

[20] John of the Cross, *The Ascent of Mt. Carmel*, book 3, chapter 22.

and the confidence God wants us to have in the individual and ecclesial sources of this understanding.

The sixth basic attitude is a pervasive spirit of thanksgiving. Because of its importance it deserves to be discussed at greater length.

REMAINING IN A STATE OF THANKSGIVING

"*Give thanks in all circumstances; for this is the will of God in Christ Jesus for you*" (1 Thess 5:18). St. Paul's exhortation to the Thessalonians repeats a theme often heard in the psalms: "*I will bless the Lord at all times; praise shall be always in my mouth*" (Ps 34:2). Thanksgiving is not just one form of prayer to be practiced now and then. It should be a fundamental attitude of heart, a disposition of life, a way of orienting one's entire life.

But it is not so easy. The scandal of evil, suffered by oneself or a loved one—these things undermine an attitude of praise. I recall something I heard said years ago by a young Jewish and Catholic philosopher, Fabrice Hadjadj, during a "literary café" in Paris. The question was this: "After Auschwitz, is it still possible to praise and bless the Lord?" He answered:

If after the horrors of the Nazis, we, the believers, ceased to love God and bless him, that would simply mean that Hitler had won. Everyone is free to react as

82

he sees proper, but as far as I am concerned, I do not want to leave the victory to Hitler, so therefore I want to continue to bless God all the length of my life, whatever happens!

Praise expresses the confidence that love is stronger than hate, light stronger than darkness, and the end of history will not be the triumph of evil but the victory of the good. Jesus said to the medieval mystic Julian of Norwich: "Sin is inevitable, but all will end up well!"[21] Evil is nothingness—the absence of being—at its heart. Goodness alone has eternal value.

THE SANCTIFICATION OF THE NAME

This call to bless the name of God in all circumstances is unquestionably the most important and difficult one, but it is also the most beautiful. It ennobles the human race and enables us most fully to realize our dignity and our freedom. Someone faced with a disaster that could lead him to believe God had forgotten his promises and life was meaningless, who can nevertheless exclaim, "Blessed be the name of the Lord!" is making the greatest act of freedom and love conceivable. Suddenly he has transcended the egoism and narrowness of human mediocrity.

[21] Julian of Norwich, *A Book of Showings* (Cerf, 1992), 105.

This is the vocation of Israel: *Kiddoush ha Shem*, the sanctification of the name of God. It is why the Adversary of God has so often assaulted it. The horrors of World War II can be endlessly deplored, but they do not take away the moving grandeur of that multitude of pious Jews from all over Central Europe who went to the ovens of death reciting the *Shema* Israel. Here was a multitudinous echo of the voice of Job, who, rather than cursing God, cried out: "*The Lord gave and the Lord has taken away; blessed be the name of the Lord!*" (Job 1:21). We Christians should adopt this vocation of Israel each day as we pray, "Hallowed be thy name!" It is our privilege and our duty to bless the name of God all the days of our lives. At the end of her life, Thérèse of Lisieux said: "This word of Job: '*Even if God kills me, I will still hope in him!*' delighted me since my childhood."[22]

When the Heavenly Father's children respond to this call to bless the name of God, they raise an impregnable rampart against the forces of evil. Psalm 8 expresses this beautifully:

O Lord, our Lord, how majestic is thy name in all the earth! Thou whose glory above the heavens is chanted by the mouth of babes and infants, thou hast founded a bulwark because of thy foes, to still the enemy and the avenger (Ps 8:1–2).

[22] At the same time she specifies something that is reassuring: "It took a long time to achieve this degree of abandonment." *Last Interviews*, July 7.

The greatest act of charity one can do for others is to encourage them to live in faith and hope. To praise God is a veritable food for the soul.

> My soul is feasted as with marrow and fat, and my mouth praises thee with joyful lips, when I think of thee upon my bed, and meditate on thee in the watches of the night (Ps 63:5–6).

Here is a powerful way to grow in humility—to renounce claiming merit for ourselves and acknowledge that everything good and beautiful in life comes from the generosity of God's love. As Father Raniero Cantalamessa, preacher of the pontifical household, says, "Praise immolates and destroys man's pride; he who praises God makes a sacrifice of something that is all-pleasing to God: mankind's self-praise. The extraordinary purifying power of prayer resides in this. Humility is hidden in praise."

VINDICATION OR GRATITUDE?

Praising and thanking God also helps people give up victimhood and accept responsibility. This tendency to see oneself as a victim is very common today.

Self-anointed victims spend their time complaining, asserting, and demanding. Since they have no confidence in God, they regard difficulty or suffering as somebody's mistake, if not an outright injustice. Their ideal is a life of endless gratification, with no sorrows or struggles. When put to the test, they look for someone to blame, someone to pay for the suffering. All else failing, they blame the government for what troubles them: as if the state should or even could guarantee everyone a painless existence!

One consequence of this is the emergence of a litigious society. Yes, people do sometimes have a right to seek reparations in court. But today it is common for someone who suffers something at the hands of someone else—even a member of the family—to haul the guilty party before a judge instead of confidently and responsibly facing the difficult situation, forgiving the wrong, and shouldering his burdens for himself. In the long run, this way of acting undermines life in society, by spreading the poison of mistrust.

Praise and gratitude are the great remedies for the mentality of victimhood. Instead of complaining or seeking vindication, we are led to the acceptance of life as it comes to us, even with its weight of suffering and difficulties. We come to understand that the challenge before us is not to change our lives but to change our attitude toward life, from caution and accusation to acceptance and confidence. We learn to welcome life with faith as a gift, even though it is different from what we expected. We discover that real life is far more beautiful and rich than the life of our daydreams.

This is a fundamental spiritual principle, found in the Gospel. Jesus speaks these mysterious words:

> I tell you, that to every one who has will more be given; but from him who has not, even what he has will be taken away (Lk 19:26).

In this way he proclaims one of the most important laws of life. Someone filled with resentment and unhappiness, bitter that life is not as it should be, will be deeply disillusioned. On the other hand, people who are glad for what they have received, and thank God for what befalls them will receive still more, until finally being overwhelmed by God's generosity.

I often meet people constantly at war with life. They are never satisfied and, whatever happens, feel that things should be other than they are. Their lives are spent waging futile crusades.

At the root of this way of thinking lies unconscious anger, a kind of spite. Such feelings can energize people for a while, so that they appear to be champions of generosity and justice. But in the end it doesn't work, for in the long term fruitfulness comes only from love. People who suffer in this way may need psychological help, and the practice of gratitude and praise is sure to be beneficial. When gratitude is the most fundamental disposition of one's heart, one is able to repeat Mary's words and mean them.

> My soul magnifies the Lord, and my spirit rejoices in
> God my Savior, for he has regarded the low estate of
> his handmaiden. For behold, henceforth all genera-
> tions will call me blessed (Lk 1:46–48).

Let us ask the Virgin of the Magnificat to help us acquire this attitude as our own.

I believe that someone able to live in a permanent state of thanksgiving will very quickly become a saint. Here is the most powerful spiritual attitude for purifying the heart and opening it to divine action. Evil has no hold on a heart filled with thanksgiving.

To sum up then: Just as mistrust and the desire for revenge close us to God's calls and gifts, so do gratitude and confidence allow us to discern and welcome them. The highest expression of this gratitude is the celebration of the Eucharist, the fullest act of thanksgiving, in which the Church joins in the thanksgiving of Christ who blessed his Father for the abundance of his love and goodness. As Pope John Paul II said, the Eucharist is given to us "so that our life, like that of Mary, may be entirely a *magnificat*."[23]

---

[23] *Ecclesia de Eucharistia*, no. 50.

•• 5 ••

OBEDIENCE TO OTHERS
AND TO THE HOLY SPIRIT

"I will instruct you and teach you the way you should go; I will counsel you with my eye upon you.

—Ps 32:8

Up to now we have considered two important ways in which God's calls reach us: the Word of God and the events of life. Now I want briefly to speak of two other ways: the requests of others and the interior movements of the Holy Spirit. Much that already has been said applies also to them.

THE REQUESTS OF OTHERS

Obviously, not every request made to us is a call from God. Some requests are inappropriate, even bad. We are entitled, perhaps obligated, to say no to them.

Very often, though, requests are media through which God invites us to grow in love. They shake us up a bit and force us out of our narrowness. The needs of others and their requests, whether these are silent or expressed, often transmit God's call and promise rich rewards to those who generously respond.

But what constitutes a generous response is not always easy to say. There are no hard and fast rules that fit every case.

Sometimes laziness or egoism close us to what others ask. When that happens, we deny ourselves beautiful opportunities to live more intensely. Human beings cannot fully realize their potential without bonding with others, entering into alliances, promising and welcoming fidelity—fidelity that may sometimes be costly but is our only escape from the trap of egocentrism. This clashes with secular ideology, which holds that all ties to others—the marriage bond is an example—are infringements on individual autonomy. But the truth is very different. The bond of fidelity is an essential part of genuine freedom.[1]

Excessive dependency on other people's expectations and demands also is common. Psychological factors like fear or a need for approval, or a distorted understanding of what charity means, drive some individuals to suppose that they must say yes to everyone and everything, and please everybody from morning to

---

[1] On the subject of conjugal engagement see the wonderful book of Xavier Lacroix, *Of Flesh and the Word, Founding a Family* (Bayard, 2007), chapter 3 in particular: *Why Grow Old Together?*

night. The result is an eclipse of personality, neglect of their own needs, and bitterness instead of love. True, there can be no happiness without self-giving, but it must be genuine giving—freely chosen, disinterested, and proceeding from a certain healthful abundance on the part of the giver.

AMBIGUITIES OF SELF-GIVING

I repeat, there is no true happiness except in self-giving done out of love. "*It is more blessed to give than to receive*," Jesus said (Acts 20:35). We have all experienced this. It is good and necessary to receive love; but in the end the love that makes us happy is not so much the love we receive as it is the love we give. This is the promise of the Gospel:

> But when you give a feast, invite the poor, the maimed, the lame, the blind, and you will be blessed, because they cannot repay you. You will be repaid at the resurrection of the just (Lk 14:13–14).

Still, self-giving is not always so simple in practice. People sometimes give generously of themselves, without experiencing the happiness promised by the Gospel. Instead they encounter sorrow, fatigue, and frustration. Their own needs are forgotten; they themselves are ignored. We have all heard a generous person explode with anger and exclaim. "I'm fed up with waiting on everyone else, with having to do all the dirty work, with being taken for granted and never so much as hearing 'thank you'!"

Self-giving can end like that when it is not freely chosen or when it is chosen out of some motive other than disinterested love—fear of saying no and not being accepted, emotional dependence, a perfectionist streak rooted in pride, a sense of indebtedness, the notion that to save others we need to please them, or else the desire to teach others a lesson by shaming them. There is even such a thing as calculated generosity that resembles a kind of unconscious bargaining: I will give myself to you, provided you give me the emotional gratification or the ego boost that I crave. It is important to examine our motives and rid ourselves of such imperfect ones, so that our self-giving can become truly free and disinterested.

THE TRUE DIFFERENCE BETWEEN GIVING AND RECEIVING

No less important, but more difficult, is grasping the real difference between giving and receiving in order that our self-giving may be a source of joy. Always giving and never receiving sooner or later ends in frustration. People need encouragement and moments of pleasure and happiness.

Yet a thousand gratifications do not of themselves add up to one experience of genuine happiness, and pursuing all the physical satisfaction possible is the surest path to unhappiness. Nor does calculating help: "I will give only when I have received." Someone who acts in this way soon falls prey to the compulsion to worry and weigh, forgetting that often it is frequently in the very act of giving that we receive. Accepting God's call to plunge into some enterprise beyond our strength, we receive the grace we need—grace we did not have before.

While it is reasonable to refrain from self-giving that is forced or frustrating, the opposite extreme also is possible. Today's popular media are constantly screaming "Take care of yourself, make yourself happy, look out for number one." And it is true that some people do neglect their own needs. But people who heed this advice and no other are likely to become self-absorbed to the point of having no interest in life except themselves and their own well being.

Working out the right relationship between giving and receiving is not a matter of striking a well-honed balance between what I give others and what comes back to me. It is expressed instead in a somewhat enigmatic statement from the Gospel.

When you give alms, do not let your left hand know what your right is doing, so that your almsgiving may

93

be secret. And your Father who sees in secret will
repay you (Mt 6:3–4).

Here is the Gospel paradox. To find the holy balance
between giving and receiving, do not look for it, but
leave it up to the Father!

Our Father in Heaven knows what we need. Our
part is to give without worrying about whether we will
receive in return. But we must also learn to receive with
simplicity and freedom, without asking whether we are
worthy or exactly how to share what we have received.
These questions are for God in the light of his unfath-
omable love.

Learning to love means seeing ever more clearly
that the fundamental spiritual attitude—and paradoxi-
cally the most difficult—is openness to receiving. It is
fundamental because it is God who loves us first. It is
difficult because it requires us to have much confidence
and humility, and to let ourselves be loved.

Certainly we must take our lives in our own hands in
a responsible, active way. But we must have this filial attitude, too. The whole of the spiritual life is an appren-
ticeship in childlike trust and receptivity. This spiritual
receptivity is learned little by little, in a process that
never ends. For this is no less than the poverty of spirit
of which the Beatitudes speak (Mt 5:1). The proud person is unable to receive, because pride does not allow it.
Only the humble person knows how to receive.

As for giving, the source for that must be sought in God and not one's self. Too often we wish to give according to our criteria, our wisdom, our strength. And then we wear out quickly. The Scriptures make this promise:

> Even youths shall faint and be weary, and young men shall fall exhausted; but they who wait for the Lord shall renew their strength, they shall mount up with wings like eagles, they shall run and not be weary, they shall walk and not faint (Isa 40:30–31).

OBEDIENCE

Let us turn now to the spiritual value of obedience. This is a complex matter and one very poorly understood in modern times. I shall not treat it in detail, but only make a few remarks.

The idea and practice of obedience have undergone a long evolution in the realm of ecclesiastical and religious life. This development has been in the direction of things like dialogue, respect for others, and collegiality. The exhortations to blind obedience of the past are no longer acceptable, and that's probably for the best.

The danger now, however, lies in going too far in the other direction, and regarding obedience of any sort as by definition alienating or dishonorable, an assault on the rights of the person. The criteria used in defining cults in today's France place even Carmelite and Benedictine monasteries at risk! Submitting to a superior is considered shameful—a mortal sin against self-realization and individual autonomy. To be sure, people still submit to authority at work or behind the wheel of a car, but to do so is an abomination.

And yet it is as true today as ever that the request of someone exercising legitimate authority in the Church in an appropriate manner should normally be considered as an authentic expression of God's call, even if the request doesn't suit what you and I may have in mind. I have often had that experience. Even though superiors have their own limitations and sometimes err, ecclesial or religious obedience lived in love and faith remains a reliable, fruitful guide. And one that is liberating as well, because it prevents us from isolating ourselves in our own projects and personal preferences. Such obedience is testimony that our lives are no longer simply our own but have been placed in God's hands. It witnesses to the fundamental truth that authentic liberty is the liberty found in Christ.

It is worth reflecting on the advice St. Paul gives Christian slaves—namely, that they should submit to their masters, something we have trouble understanding today. But the advice was at once realistic and prophetic. Realistic, because a rebellion by slaves in the Roman Empire would have risked a reenactment of the repression after Spartacus' revolt, when six thousand slaves were crucified along the Via Appia between Rome and Capua. Prophetic, because more urgent than promoting social reforms, which would come sooner or later anyway, was giving witness that the true dignity and liberty of the individual are not found in social status but in Christ. Paul was audacious enough to ask this madness of Christian slaves: that they extend obedience to their masters, "*as to Christ*,"[2] and thereby testify to them that, whether one be slave or free, what really matters is the new life in Christ and the freedom to love that it brings.

Much could be said about ecclesiastical obedience and the circumstances that make it either legitimate or abusive, about misuses of authority and psychological hang-ups. These are important subjects, but they are not my subject here. I wish simply to make the point that the a priori rejection of authority is not the way to maturity and freedom. The requests that others make of us, even the unexpected or disturbing ones, often carry with them an offer of life and fruitfulness, while permanently closing one's ears to these requests ends in sterility.

THE SPIRIT'S DESIRES

The inspirations and desires that the Holy Spirit causes to spring up in hearts make up an extremely important

[2] See Eph 6:5–9.

medium by which God's calls reach people. Having written elsewhere about this subject,[3] I shall not say much about it here, but it is an essential aspect of the spiritual life. The promptings that originate with the Holy Spirit may concern either humble matters or lofty ones, but it is always very fruitful to respond to them. St. Faustina Kōwalska,[4] canonized by Pope John Paul II in April 2000, called faithfulness to the inspirations of the Holy Spirit the shortest way to sainthood.[5]

The Word, the events of life, and the motions of the Spirit are not three independent channels, used by God to communicate with us as circumstances dictate. Every call necessarily involves all three, with the emphasis on one or the other.

Therefore, these reflections on the motions of the Spirit are directly linked to what has already been said. Interior desires and movements of the Spirit are often awakened or nourished by the Word of God. The practice of *lectio divina* and the experience of being moved by Holy Scripture are excellent instruction in being sensitive to God's inspiration. On the other hand, it is often interior motions that enable people to perceive the call present in some event. The

[3] *In the School of the Holy Spirit* (Scepter Publishers, Inc., 2007).

[4] Polish nun (1905–1938), canonized the Sunday after Easter 2000. She received much wisdom from the Lord concerning divine mercy, including the invitation that this Sunday become the feast of divine mercy.

[5] *Little Journal of Sr. Faustina*, ed. Jules Hovine, 142.

Spirit often makes us know in our hearts what ought to be done in a particular situation. Often, too, the Spirit interiorly disposes us to obey God's will present in some exterior request.

All too often, though, people refuse or ignore what the Spirit asks of them. There are many reasons: shallow prayer, failure to listen interiorly,[6] dread of silence, and a craving for worldly noise and agitation as distractions from what is happening in one's soul. Anxieties and attachments render people incapable of welcoming the promptings of grace. Thus they deny themselves an interior source of vitality and fruitfulness and forfeit the promise of Scripture:

> And the Lord will guide you continually, and satisfy your desire with good things, and make your bones strong; and you shall be like a watered garden, like a spring of water, whose waters fail not (Isa 58:11).

THE DESIRE OF MANKIND AND THE WILL OF GOD

The Spirit educates desire. Christians have sometimes considered human desire to be so opposed to God's will that the two things could only be contradictory. On a deeper level, however, they are meant to converge. Not

---

[6] "To listen is first of all to make silence, around us and in us, in order to be able to be attentive to what is addressed to us." Jean-Louis Chrétien, *Call and Response* (Editions de Minuit, 1992), 32.

only do human beings want happiness, it is their vocation. God's call and the deepest desire of the human heart go hand in hand. God's invitation to give ourselves out of love corresponds to the desire of our hearts. As John Paul II says:

> The inclination to giving is etched in the intimate depths of the human heart; every person feels the desire to relate to others and is fully realized when giving freely to others.[7]

The spiritual life would be unlivable if negation and repression were the only legitimate responses to our desires. But the spiritual path is not a way of negation but an education of desire: progressively learning to leave superficial desires behind in order to let the deepest desire emerge, the one that carries the call addressed to us by God. Other desires come from our wounded psyches, or are imposed on us by others or by the world. It is the work of the Holy Spirit to wed together the call of God and the desires of humankind, either by leading us to desire what God wants to give us, or by overcoming superficial desires. This is God's promise to Jeremiah:

> Behold, the days are coming, says the Lord, when I will make a new covenant with the house of Israel and

[7] Lenten Message, 2003.

the house of Judah, not like the covenant which I made with their fathers when I took them by the hand to bring them out of the land of Egypt, my covenant which they broke, though I was their husband, says the Lord. But this is the covenant which I will make with the house of Israel after those days, says the Lord: I will put my law within them, and I will write it upon their hearts; and I will be their God, and they shall be my people. And no longer shall each man teach his neighbor and each his brother, saying, "Know the Lord," for they shall all know me, from the least of them to the greatest, says the Lord; for I will forgive their iniquity, and I will remember their sin no more (Jer 31:31–34).

In the New Covenant doing God's will in fidelity to his call is not something externally imposed. It arises spontaneously and freely as the expression of the heart's deepest desire. But we must be realistic. To educate one's desires is long, difficult work requiring struggle and renunciation inasmuch as the wound of sin has left desire disoriented and fragmented.[8]

---

[8] These considerations are important for discernment. See, for example, Andre Louf, *Grace Can Do More*, chapter 9 (DDB). As a matter of vocational discernment, it is safe to say that a call that cannot be embraced altogether freely because it does not resonate with the deep desire of the heart is not a call from God.

CONCLUSION

THE GOD OF ALL THAT IS BEAUTIFUL

Now I wish to reflect on calling and beauty.[1] The two words are close in Greek: kalos means beautiful, *kalein* means to call.[2] There are deep harmonies between what we have said about God who calls and the mystery of beauty. Dionysius the Areopagite says: "God calls (*kaloun*) all things to himself, that is why he is called *kalos* (beauty)."[3]

Beauty calls—it summons. It leaves no person indifferent; it incites a desire. "God calls to himself all things as the desirable calls to itself desire."[4] This is an invitation to a response: to admire and love in return the beauty that calls us in manifesting itself. One does not do this on one's own. The movement that draws one toward what is beautiful and causes one to give thanks does not come from oneself but from beauty.

[1] These reflections are inspired by the philosophical volume of Jean-Louis Chrétien, *Call and Response* (Editions de Minuit, 1992).

[2] We need, especially today, to discover (as so many saints and mystics in the past did) God as beauty. A renewal of Christian art is essential.

[3] Denis, *De divinis nominibus*, IV, 7. Cited by Jean-Louis Chrétien, op. cit.

[4] Ulrich de Strasbourg, theologian from the thirteenth century. Cited in op. cit., 27.

Purity, disinterestedness, and generosity are present in true beauty, as they are in God. The beauty of something beautiful is not for itself but for those who contemplate it and rejoice in it. Narcissistic beauty is contemptible.

We can assign no limits to the call to love addressed to us by the one who is Beauty itself. This call, which is also a call of truth and goodness,[5] asks a total giving of our very selves. Infinitely generous, it also summons forth limitless generosity in the person who is open to it. The right measure of love for God is to love him without measure. And in thus losing ourselves, we find ourselves. "The call that beauty directs to us also calls us to ourselves."[6]

I HAVE CALLED YOU BY YOUR NAME

The deepest origin, ultimate synthesis, and fullest realization of everything said so far are found in the mystery of Christ. Finally, in fact, there is only one word by which the Father calls us: the one he communicates through his Son. St. John of the Cross says the Father has but a single word to say to us—the Son.[7] He is

---

[5] God is all at once beauty, truth, and goodness. We focus here on beauty, since it is perhaps especially insofar as they are beautiful that truth and goodness draw us in.

[6] Chrétien, op. cit., 23.

[7] "In giving us his Son as he has, his Son who is his unique Word—for there is no other—God has said everything to us at one time by this Word." *Ascent of Mount Carmel*, book two, chapter 22.

God's greatest gift to humanity, God's most important call. "*So if there is any encouragement in Christ, any incentive of love, any participation in the Spirit, any affection and sympathy, complete my joy by being of the same mind, having the same love, being in full accord and of one mind*" (Phil. 2:1–2).

Christ sums up everything that was said in creation, everything communicated to the people of Israel. In his Incarnation and Resurrection, he is the definitive word to which nothing can be added. He tells us everything about God and about man. One Word of inexhaustible richness. St. John of the Cross, speaking of the mysteries of Christ, compares them to caverns or mines containing endless treasures awaiting discovery:

> The holy doctors have done well in discovering, and the worthy souls have done well in tasting, the marvelous things in this life, both of them expressing only a very small part of these things. What an abyss to plumb is Christ! Here is an abundant mine containing numberless rich veins; we can dig here forever, without ever reaching the end. . . . We discover new veins in every direction that reveal other riches. This is what St. Paul said, speaking of Christ: "*Christ, in whom are hidden all the treasures of wisdom and knowledge*" (Col 2:3).

In the end, God's many calls have their source in a single call. It is the call to welcome the mystery of

Christ and let ourselves be illuminated and transformed by him.

The first call we discussed—the call to live expressed in creation—is already, mysteriously, a call in Christ. All things are created in him, by him, and for him.

> He is the image of the invisible God, the firstborn of all creation. For in him were created all things in heaven and on earth, the visible and the invisible, whether thrones or dominions or principalities or powers; all things were created through him and for him. He is before all things, and in him all things hold together (Col 1:15–17).

The call of creation that comes to us is a call to be fully human, something that can be realized only in Christ. For he is the only fully realized human being, the one who corresponds entirely to God's will. As the Second Vatican Council says: "Whoever follows Christ the perfect man, becomes himself more a man."[9]

The baptismal call is also a call to Christ, but more clearly and explicitly so. Through baptism, we receive a new gift, divine life, and a new call, to make a personal decision to follow Christ and be transformed in him.

All the different callings in the Church—marriage, priesthood, consecrated life, etc.—are infused with the grace of baptism and are calls to live a facet of Christ's

[9] *Gaudium et Spes*, 41, 1.

mystery: Christ the spouse, Christ the priest, "Christ in contemplation on the mountain, or proclaiming the kingdom of God to the multitudes, or healing the sick and maimed and converting sinners to a good life, or blessing the children and doing good to all men, always in obedience to the will of the Father who sent him."[10]

Each of God's interventions in one's life—through Scripture, life's events, the movements of the Spirit, the various media of grace described in this book—has no goal except to propel one toward this identification with Christ, which is the ultimate meaning of human existence. Human beings are called to love, and love is learned only at the school of Christ. *Have this mind among yourselves, which is yours in Christ Jesus*" (Phil 2:5). "*Take my yoke upon you, and learn from me; for I am gentle and lowly in heart, and you will find rest for your souls, for my yoke is easy, and my burden is light*" (Mt 11:29).

The term *call* has two meanings: to name or designate, and to invite. These meanings are joined in the mystery of Christ. In responding to his invitation to be converted and follow him, we find our true identity and receive the new name that tells us who we are and what our mission is.

He who has an ear, let him hear what the Spirit says to the churches. To him who conquers I will give some of

[10] Expressions used by the Second Vatican Council about religious life. *Lumen Gentium*, no. 46.

the hidden manna, and I will give him a white stone,
with a new name written on the stone which no one
knows except him who receives it (Rev 2:17).

This "new name" does not negate or cancel one's
old name, which is one's identity in simply being created. Rather, the new name restores and renews the old,
rescues it from fixation upon the self, reveals its deepest
meaning, and in the end brings it to fulfillment.

Appendix

PRACTICAL ADVICE
FOR *LECTIO DIVINA*

"The Scripture is neither closed such that it is discouraging, nor acces-
sible such that it becomes banal. The more we frequent it, the less we
grow tired of it, the more we meditate on it, the more we love it."[1]

I want to offer some advice for practicing *lectio divina*.
We have seen earlier how necessary it is that our hearts
embrace the Word of God. This happens first and
foremost in the liturgical assembly, when the Holy
Scriptures are proclaimed and commented on. But it
remains necessary that each of us take moments to
listen to the Word of God and be "called, oriented, and
fashioned" by it, in the words of Pope John Paul II.

The suggestions that follow should be put into practice very freely and flexibly. Everyone needs to discover
for himself the best way of integrating the reading of
Scripture into his life.

---

[1] St. Gregory the Great, *Moralia in Job*, XX, 1,1. Cited in an address of Pope
John Paul II on October 20, 1997, the day after he proclaimed of St. Thérèse
of Lisieux a doctor of the Church.

To the extent possible, some time should be dedicated to prayerful reading of the Word, thus continuing the rich monastic tradition of *lectio divina*. This is not continuous reading of the Bible, a chapter a day perhaps, with the aim of getting through as much of it as possible. Nor is it time spent in Bible study and exegesis. People with the opportunity will find it very beneficial to study the Bible using a variety of tools: courses, the study of biblical languages, dictionaries, concordances, commentaries, and various techniques for interpreting the text (historical, archeological, semiotic).

Such studies can be a support for *lectio divina*, but *lectio* itself is something different. It is meditative reading of the Scriptures done with simplicity, prayer, and faith, with a goal of hearing what the Lord wants to say to one today in order to be enlightened and transformed by it.

What is crucial in this enterprise is not how much one knows but the attitude of one's heart—an attitude of thirst for God, confidence that he wants to speak to one, and a great desire for conversion. Here is the great secret of *lectio*. Reading Scripture will be far more fruitful for one in whom the desire of conversion is strong. Many simple, unlettered people have received great light and powerful encouragement from Holy Scripture because they were confident in encountering the living Word of God. St. Thérèse herself is one of many examples.

Much of the advice that applies to prayer applies also to *lectio divina*: the importance of perseverance, accepting arid periods, the fundamental role of faith and hope, etc. Indeed, *lectio divina* is the most ancient, most universal, and most practiced of all the "methods of prayer."[2] Done in the manner to be described, it is the best entry into a life of prayer. Here, then, are recommendations.

WHAT TIME IS BEST?

If you can, it is good to take time every day to meditate on the Word. Busy as we are, we find time daily to nourish our bodies, so why not our souls? Ideally, morning is best, for then our spirits are most fresh and best disposed, not yet burdened by the accumulated worries of the day. Psalm 90 says: "*Satisfy us in the morning with thy steadfast love, that we may rejoice and be glad all our days*" (Ps 90:14). And Isaiah: "*Morning by morning he wakens my ear to hear*" (Is 50:4).

To do *lectio divina* in the morning testifies that the most important thing in one's life is to heed God. *Lectio* places one in an attitude of listening extending through

---

[2] I use the word prayer here in the sense that it has taken in Western tradition since the sixteenth century: silent personal prayer, practiced regularly for a determined time, whose goal is to make us enter into communion with God and unite us to him. See my work: *Time for God, A Guide to Mental Prayer* (Scepter Publishers, Inc., 2008).

the course of the day. That said, it is clear that many people cannot take time in the morning and must find other moments for them. If they thirst for God, he can speak with him just the same.

How long? A quarter of an hour at least. A half-hour or forty-five minutes is better.

WHAT TEXT TO MEDITATE ON?

The possibilities are many. One can meditate for days on a particular text—one of the gospels, a letter of Paul, or something else. I know a married man, the father of a family, who takes time to pray with the Word of God every day. He has stayed with the Gospel of John for two or three years.

Still, my advice to beginners is to use the texts chosen by the Church for the Mass of the day. This has the advantage of joining us with the universal Church and its liturgical calendar and preparing us for the Eucharist if we participate in it that day. Moreover, in this way three well-chosen texts are available to us (first reading, psalm, Gospel), so that there is less chance of having to wrestle with something too dry or too difficult. Practicing *lectio* by immersing oneself simultaneously in several texts also enables one to see the profound unity of the Scriptures. It is a great joy to discover how scripture texts very different by style, era, or composition complement one another.

When interpreting Scripture, sages of rabbinic tradition love to make the richness of the texts leap out by "stringing necklaces." The pearls are verses from different parts of Scripture—the Torah, the Prophets, the Psalms, and wisdom writings. Jesus did the same after the Resurrection for the two disciples on the road to Emmaus (Lk 24:27 and 24:44). This tradition of drawing together different texts that shed light on one another was followed by the Fathers of the Church and is practiced by spiritual writers up to this day.

HOW TO PROCEED IN A CONCRETE WAY

As has been emphasized, the profit to be drawn from *lectio divina* has more to do with interior dispositions than technique. One should not launch directly into reading, but should allow time to get ready by adopting a prayerful disposition of faith and desire for God. Here are some steps.

1. As with any time of prayer, it is best to draw back and place oneself in God's presence. Set aside worries and distractions. As Mary of Bethany knew, what is necessary is to put oneself at the feet of the Lord and listen to his word.[3] This means situating oneself in the present moment, something that is

3 Cf. the story of Martha and Mary, Lk 10:38–42.

sometimes quite difficult to do. Turning to the body
and its sensations may help. The body has its short-
comings, but it has an advantage over thought in
being always in the present, while thoughts often
flit back and forth between the past and the future.
God is encountered only in the present moment,
and the body and its sensations help situate a person there. Often, then, bodily preparation should
come before reading: closing one's eyes, relaxing
(flex the shoulders and other muscles that may be
tense), breathe slowly but deeply, be aware of the
body's contact with its surroundings—the ground
beneath one's feet, the seat one occupies, the table
one's arms rest upon, the hands holding the Bible
or other book to be read. The first contact with the
Word must be physical. Touching is already a sort of
listening. Does not St. John say: "*What was from the
beginning, what we have heard, what we have seen with
our eyes, what we looked upon and touched with our
hands concerns the Word of life*" (1 Jn 1:1)?

2. Once sufficiently relaxed, in contact with the body
and situated in the present moment, one must turn
one's heart toward God, thanking him for this
moment in which he will join one by his Word,
asking him to open one's mind to understand the
Scriptures as he opened the minds of his disciples
(Lk 24:44). Especially he should be asked to convert

one's heart, condemn sinful compromises, enlighten and transform one to be more responsive to his divine project for one's life.

3. Take as long as necessary to be well disposed, for it is essential. Then open your eyes and begin to read. Read slowly, applying the intelligence and the heart to what is read and meditating on it.

"Meditate," in the biblical tradition, signifies not so much reflecting as repeating and ruminating. It is more physical than intellectual at first. Do not hesitate to repeat a passage many times, since this often is how what God wishes to say by it today will emerge. Reflective intelligence obviously has a role to play. One can question the text: What does it say about God? About myself? What good news does it contain? What invitation? If a verse seems obscure, the use of notes or a commentary may help—but be careful not to turn *lectio* into intellectual study.

Feel free to spend time on a verse that takes on a particular significance for you. Dialogue with God about it. This kind of reading is meant to become prayer. Give thanks for a passage that encourages, ask God's help for one that summons to a difficult conversion, etc. At certain moments, if the grace is given, stop reading and pause in a more contemplative attitude of prayer that may be simple admiration of the beauty that God has made us find in the text: his sweetness, his majesty, his faithfulness, the splendor of what he did in Christ, and invite one simply to contemplate that and give thanks. The ultimate goal of *lectio* is not to cover vast quantities of text, but to introduce us to this attitude of contemplative awe that deeply nourishes faith, hope, and love. It is not always granted, but when it is, stop the reading and be content with the simple, loving presence of the mystery the text has unveiled.

What has just been said covers the four stages of *lectio divina* according to the tradition of the Middle Ages: *lectio* (reading), *meditatio* (meditation), *oratio* (prayer), and *contemplatio* (contemplation). They do not necessarily occur in sequence, but are particular modes of experience. The first three depend on human activity, but the fourth is a gift of grace. We must desire it and welcome it, but it is not always given to us. Moreover, as I have said, there can be times of aridity, of dryness, as in any prayer. Never be discouraged. What is sought will be found in the end.

While meditating, it is good to make written notes about words that touch us particularly. Use a notebook for this purpose. Writing helps make the Word penetrate more deeply into one's heart and memory.

Once the time for *lectio* is up, thank the Lord for the moments spent with him, and ask him for grace to keep the Word in your heart, as the Virgin Mary did, and to put into practice the enlightenment received in meditation.

I want to conclude with a beautiful passage of Matta el-Maskin, the contemporary Egyptian monk who has fostered a magnificent spiritual renewal in Coptic monasticism.

Meditation is not simply vocal reading in depth, it also means silent repetition of the Word numerous times, with an ever-growing deepening until the heart is embraced by divine fire. That is illustrated by what David said in Psalm 39: "*My heart smoldered within me. In my thoughts a fire blazed up.*" Here the secret line appears that links practice and effort to grace and divine fire. The mere fact of meditating several times on the Word of God, slowly and tranquilly, will build, through the mercy of God and his grace, to the embrace of the heart! Thus, meditation becomes the first, normal link between sincere effort at prayer and the gifts of God and his ineffable grace. For this reason, meditation has been considered the first and most important of the heart's degrees of prayer, from which mankind can lift itself to the fervor of the Spirit, and live there as long as life lasts.[4]

[4] Matta El Maskin, *The Experience of God in the Life of Prayer* (Cerf), 48.